How to Speak so People Listen

PEARSON

At Pearson, we believe in learning – all kinds of learning for all kinds of people. Whether it's at home, in the classroom or in the workplace, learning is the key to improving our life chances.

That's why we're working with leading authors to bring you the latest thinking and the best practices, so you can get better at the things that are important to you. You can learn on the page or on the move, and with content that's always crafted to help you understand quickly and apply what you've learned.

If you want to upgrade your personal skills or accelerate your career, become a more effective leader or more powerful communicator, discover new opportunities or simply find more inspiration, we can help you make progress in your work and life.

Pearson is the world's leading learning company. Our portfolio includes the Financial Times, Penguin, Dorling Kindersley, and our educational business, Pearson International.

Every day our work helps learning flourish, and wherever learning flourishes, so do people.

To learn more please visit us at: www.pearson.com/uk

How to Speak so People Listen

Grab their attention and get your message heard

Mike Clayton

Harlow, England • London • New York • Boston • San Francisco • Toronto • Sydney • Auckland • Singapore • Hong Kong
Tokyo • Seoul • Taipei • New Delhi • Cape Town • São Paulo • Mexico City • Madrid • Amsterdam • Munich • Paris • Milan

PEARSON EDUCATION LIMITED
Edinburgh Gate
Harlow CM20 2JE
United Kingdom
Tel: +44 (0)1279 623623
Web: www.pearson.com/uk

First published 2013 (print and electronic)

© Pearson Education Limited 2013 (print and electronic)

The right of Mike Clayton to be identified as author of this work has been asserted by him in accordance with the Copyright, Designs and Patents Act 1988.

Pearson Education is not responsible for the content of third-party internet sites.

ISBN: 978-0-273-78637-5 (print)
       978-0-273-78868-3 (PDF)
       978-0-273-78861-4 (ePub)

British Library Cataloguing-in-Publication Data
A catalogue record for the print edition is available from the British Library

Library of Congress Cataloging-in-Publication Data
Clayton, Mike.
  How to speak so people listen : grab their attention and get your message heard / Mike Clayton.
    pages cm
  Includes bibliographical references and index.
  ISBN 978-0-273-78637-5
  1. Communication in organizations. 2. Oral communication. 3. Interpersonal communication.
  I. Title.
  HD30.3.C53 2013
  658.4'52--dc23
                        2013024677

10 9 8 7 6 5 4 3 2 1
17 16 15 14 13

Illustrations by Toni Goffe
Cover design by David Carroll & Co

Print edition typeset in 9/13pt Helvetica Neue LT Pro Light by 30
Printed in Great Britain by Henry Ling Ltd., at the Dorset Press, Dorchester, Dorset

NOTE THAT ANY PAGE CROSS REFERENCES REFER TO THE PRINT EDITION

To Ade, a wise friend who always spoke so people listened.

Contents

About the author

Mike's job is to speak so people listen.

And it has been for more than 20 years; first as a consultant and business adviser, then as a project manager and leader with international consultancy firm Deloitte, then as an executive performance coach and trainer. Now Mike speaks to audiences large and small for much of his professional time, delivering seminars and keynotes.

And when he is not speaking, he is writing – which is a bit like speaking to one person, whom you have never met. How do you do?

Writing has become such an important part of Mike's life that perhaps a future book will be *How to Write so People will Read*. But for the time being he is focused on spoken communication: a skill, a tool, an art – and something most of us take for granted.

Mike has never taken speaking for granted, because he knows its importance. Mike also knows the value of listening; communication has always been his passion, and being listened to – and read – is a great honour.

How to Speak so People Listen is Mike's tenth book, and his sixth with Pearson.

Acknowledgements

Thank you to Toni Goffe once again for producing the illustrations for this book.

Thank you to everyone who has sat in an audience or training room listening to me.

... and thank you to Felicity for everything.

The way we speak

Part One

Thinking about speaking

Chapter One

Speech and communication are astonishing achievements that mark our species out from the rest of the animal kingdom. But often, we speak and yet people don't listen, so this chapter identifies the barriers that get in the way of communicating and the principles of how to make it work.

How often do you speak each day?

A hundred times, a thousand?

And each time you do, you hope that people will pay attention; that they will listen. Because you want to convince, influence, make a point or tell your story. And it won't work unless people listen to you.

Speaking so that people listen to you is a crucial business skill, at all stages of your career. And it is one that you will make great use of at home, among friends and in your social life too. Communicating is a vital part of being human and there is almost nothing more important. Without it, we quickly become sad, angry and depressed. Yet most of the time, you take it for granted. You speak: people listen.

But how often have you been in a meeting, had a great idea and shared it, only to find that nobody paid much attention and the meeting moved on? There you are, sat wondering, 'Why didn't anybody get what I was saying?' You know what you said was intelligent and important, yet nobody seemed to notice.

Or maybe you have had to give a presentation. You prepared carefully, covered everything and yet, after a few minutes, you feel a growing realisation that people are starting to drift away. By halfway, you are desperate to grab their attention but you don't know how and so, by the end, you are mentally exhausted and just relieved to be finished. There is desultory clapping – hardly applause – and nobody has any questions.

And when you are in a sales meeting, it can be even worse. Nothing you say seems to carry any weight with your potential client. All they seem to focus on is the same question and, by the end, you absolutely know that they are going to buy an inferior product, at an inflated price, from your weaker competitor.

Could there be a problem here?

Chances are the problem is not your idea, or your presentation subject, or your product. More likely, you've been speaking and people just don't listen to you.

That's what this book is for; to show you how to speak so people will listen. It will help you to get your message across powerfully, persuasively and compellingly, whether you are in front of a vast audience at a conference, or chatting to one person in a corridor. This book is packed with insights and tools, strategies and techniques, checklists and tips, which will ensure that when you speak, people do pay attention and really hear what you have to say.

In fact, you'll get more than that, because listening is just a start: people will listen, they will understand, they will be persuaded and they will act.

The power of speech

Speech has tremendous power in human culture: it can inspire great acts and herald terrible evils. Speech can infuse a nation's consciousness, transform the perceptions of a generation and plant indelible associations.

At a more personal level, losing the power of speech – your voice – can leave you feeling impotent in a world where we need to communicate constantly. Anyone who has lost the power of speech, either temporarily or permanently, will know the feelings of sheer frustration that accompany your efforts to be heard in a world designed around the power of speech.

Barriers to communication

The act of producing speech is only one of many barriers to fully harnessing its power; there are plenty of others:

Having something worthwhile to say

→ **Ideas:** First, you need something that makes it worthwhile for me to listen to you at all. This can be new ideas, different ways of interpreting ideas or a better approach to presenting them.

→ **Doubt:** When you are uncertain about what you want to say, you end up communicating your lack of conviction. When something is complex, you must convey its subtleties; but when you allow hesitancy into your speech, your impact will be diminished.

Getting people's attention

→ **Perception:** How are you heard? Do listeners notice you and pay attention and, if they do, do they accurately hear what you say, and do they register your message, ready to record, consider and act on it?

Putting your message across effectively

→ **Culture:** We each bring all of our cultural influences into our speech. Some of them will be alien to our listeners, and can create unwanted barriers to communicating.

→ **Language:** Even among speakers of the same language, there are linguistic differences in how we use language, such as regional accents and dialects. Different parts of society use difference sociolects, men women have subtly different genderlects, cultural sub-groups strengthen bonds with their own ethnolects, and the young move language forward, using their own chronolect. We each have a personal way of using our language; our very own idiolect.

→ **Meaning:** The meaning we take from the speech we hear is rarely precisely what the speaker intended. We filter what we hear through our experiences, prejudices, beliefs, values and labels to create our own interpretation of what we hear. So even when we hear everything that is said, in the way it was said, we fail to understand everything that was meant, in the way it was meant.

Creating the impact and results you want

→ **Emotion:** Your emotions frame your speech, creating impact when harnessed, or destroying your credibility by betraying fear, animus or undue sentimentality.

→ **Technology:** When our speech is mediated by technology, its potential power and the pitfalls increase massively. So much of today's vocal culture is transmitted via amplification, recording and broadcast, that technology has become an essential discipline for many speakers.

→ **Psychology:** To be an effective speaker, you must understand the psychology of how people hear and process what you say. When you do, that knowledge can massively boost your ability to influence and persuade, to plant memories, and to impel action. Without that knowledge, your words will just fade away.

It is a wonder we communicate at all. And, when we do, we all have habits ... many of which diffuse or distort your message. Unfortunately, it is hard to get rid of unhelpful habits so, instead, this book is about new habits you can adopt, to 'overwrite' the old ones.

From the laboratory: habits

Habits reflect patterns of activity in particular areas of the brain – predominantly the basal ganglia. Every time we repeat a habit, these patterns are strengthened and, to accompany this, we get a feeling of well-being from the brain's reward centre.

Not only do habits get stronger with time, but it also takes an act of will to overcome them, and do something else. This is effortful – the prefrontal cortex, which plans new actions, draws more energy when it functions. And it gets worse: doing something new also triggers the fear response from your amygdala, urging you to draw back from the change.

There is some good news though. You can re-programme your basal ganglia to entrench new habits, in a two-stage process.

Stage 1: Mindfulness

Notice the events that trigger habitual behaviour and pay attention to your urge to do it. Now focus on the new thoughts and behaviours that you want to replace that habit with. ▶

Stage 2: Repetition

Make a change and notice what you have done. You may not have been wholly successful in overcoming your habit, but the key is to focus on the extent of your success, rather than allow yourself to fixate on your failure. Repeat this process and gradually the new habit will start to supplant the old one.

Stage 1 is what makes the process easy. Rather than overriding the old habit, you are first concentrating on adding a new one: far less demanding. This new habit is also an unthreatening one: noticing. Stage 2 is what makes the process work. Repetition allows you to change not only your habits, but therefore how you appear to others and, maybe, who you actually are.

Making speaking work

Successful communication is all about taking responsibility for your message. It is like a four-step process, illustrated below.

As shown in the diagram below, the first step is to decide what message you want to communicate: what do you want me to understand, think or do? Then, you speak, putting your ideas across as effectively as you can, being aware of what you know about me, my cultural influences and the way I use language.

COMMUNICATION AND RESPONSE

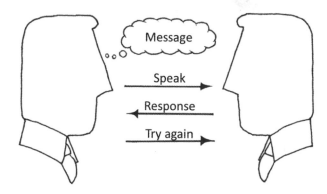

If you stop there, your ability to hold my attention and influence me will be down, in part, to good fortune. Take responsibility and notice how I react. Have I understood? What am I doing? How am I responding? Treat everything you notice as information that can help you to hone your speech and optimise it for my needs.

Now, try again. If my response was not precisely what you were aiming for, try a new way of saying it. As with so much in life, accurate perception and flexibility of approach are keys to your success.

This book is about face-to-face communication. There are many skills to master and speaking is only one. Speaking so that people will listen to you relies on all of them, so this book is really about far more than speaking:

→ Listening (the golden skill)*

→ Silence*

→ Thinking

→ Questioning

→ Posture

→ Gesture

→ Language

→ Noticing

→ Interpreting

→ Speaking*

The structure of How to Speak so People Listen

The next chapter will introduce you to how we listen and, therefore, your challenge in speaking so that people will listen. I have divided the

---

* For the deaf, listening, silence and speaking are replaced by the skills of seeing, stillness and signing. The use of sign language is as much speech as the use of vocal language, in the sense of communicating information, ideas and emotions. Unfortunately, I am not knowledgeable in this area so this book is about vocal speech: 'Whereof one cannot speak, thereof one must be silent' (Ludwig Wittgenstein).

main part of the book into two sections. Chapters 3 to 6 will give you the basic steps of:

3 How to find something to say.

4 How to get attention when you are ready to speak.

5 How to get your message across in a compelling, persuasive and way.

6 How to get powerful results by using the psychology of memory, influence and persuasion.

The following four chapters will help you to apply your new knowledge to four situations. I will give you the tools to speak so people will listen:

7 In conversations, particularly when you have a purpose in mind.

8 In complicated conversations where emotions and stakes run high.

9 In meetings, both formal and informal.

10 In public, when you are speaking to small or large audiences.

Getting started

Chapter Two

This book is about speaking: communicating your ideas, thoughts and feelings to others present, in words. But what do we mean by 'communicating'? This chapter introduces the idea that speaking so people listen is just a start – you also want them to understand, agree, remember and act. So what gets in the way of all of this? I will also introduce the idea of mental filters that transform what you say into what people hear.

Levels of speaking

My aim in this book is to help you find ways to speak more effectively. Speaking so people listen is, for me, just the first step. As you read through this book, I want you to learn how to speak in ways that are compelling, persuasive and powerful. These three concepts will help you achieve six levels of speaking.

Level 1 demands that your speaking be compelling so that people want to listen – and keep listening – and level 2 requires that you make the information easy to absorb. Levels 3 and 4 require more: that you can explain your ideas clearly and justify them to your audience. To achieve levels 5 and 6, you must also speak powerfully, using psychological and emotional cues to change the way your listeners think and act.

THE SIX LEVELS OF SPEAKING

Compelling	Level 1. How to speak so people listen
	Level 2. How to speak so people understand
Persuasive	Level 3. How to speak so people understand, as you intend them to
	Level 4. How to speak so people agree with you
Powerful	Level 5. How to speak so people remember what you want them to
	Level 6. How to speak so people think or do what you want them to

Mental filters

I could make my job easy by constraining my ambition for this book to level 1. Arguably, we are all pretty good at speaking so people listen. Humans are, fundamentally, story-telling creatures and we naturally tell and engage with stories. Whether you are at a bus stop, around a campfire, with your feet up and your nose in a book, or in front of the television screen, you spend a lot of your time enjoying stories. If you can tell a story, you can make people listen.

Story-telling is vastly under-used in business contexts

A story is a representation of the world. It is creative to the extent that it bends and stretches experience to present it in a novel way. It is instructive to the extent that it identifies and conveys universal truths or rules. And it is shorter and simpler than the real world it portrays, by selecting which information it retains and which it loses. Stories allow us to choose which perspective to take, to direct our audience where to focus and help them to identify personally with the subject.

In telling a story, you assimilate a vast amount of information about the world, you process that through your own ways of thinking, and what emerges is your representation of that world, in the form of a story. The story is not reality: it is a bent, twisted, stretched extract of the world, with gaps in your experience filled in with wisdom and guesswork. And audiences love stories because of all of that.

Your ways of thinking create **mental filters** – processes by which your brain applies your experiences, values, beliefs and prejudices to your current experience, to produce your own image of the world. Your mind selects what to focus on, deleting lots of information that it considers irrelevant. It interprets and distorts your experiences to try and fit them into familiar patterns, and when it cannot, it tries to generalise your experiences to create new patterns and templates to interpret future events. The best stories are generalisations of common experiences, selected, twisted and distorted artfully, to bring out powerful messages from which we can learn valuable lessons. The worst create equally powerful distortions of reality that can lead to poor choices.

Irena dealt with Nurdle Trading ten years ago, while at her former company. At that time, Nurdle's bonus scheme led many of its sales staff to make promises about service levels and product quality that the company could not meet. In the last five years, new management has changed the whole culture at Nurdle and created a vastly enhanced product offering too. Yet when Irena reads her team's report on which supplier to select after a competitive bid process, she rejects their finding that Nurdle is by far the best choice, despite independent testing and excellent testimonials. In Irena's mind, the samples are not representative and nobody from Nurdle can be trusted.

In this example, Irena's filters come from direct personal experiences that made a big impression on her. Filters can also arise from your upbringing and the attitudes of the people around you, from your society and culture, your values and faith, your education and training, and from your personality of course.

And our filters can shift from day to day, and even more quickly, as your mood changes. A success can predispose you to optimism and a failure can set you up to fear the slightest risk.

When you tell me a story, if it is engaging, I will listen. But as I absorb your story, my own mental filters will do their work of deforming, selecting and generalising what I hear. My understanding of your message is based on the story I create in my mind; not on the story you tell me. Speaking at level 3, so that I understand what you intend, means telling your story so well that the story I form is very much the same as yours.

STORY-TELLING

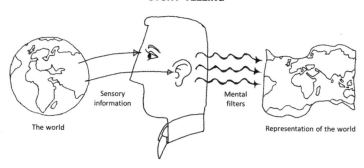

Sensory information

The world

Mental filters

Representation of the world

Phil is a capable, newly promoted manager, who still lacks confidence in his new role. When his boss Carlo suggested to Phil that he go on a more advanced management skills course, Phil thought this was a sign that Carlo thought he was failing. In fact, Carlo was pleased with his performance and thought that the more advanced training would boost Phil's confidence.

Your challenge as a speaker is immense. To communicate fully, you must engage me with compelling speech. You must help me to understand what you say and in the way you intend, by making a clear and persuasive argument.

And if you want to speak at levels 5 or 6, you must speak powerfully, so that you have an impact on the choices I will make about what to think, what to believe and how to act.

STORY-LISTENING

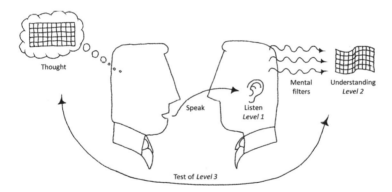

The four steps

Part Two

Get something to say

Chapter Three

People will only listen to you if you have something interesting to say. With so much stimulation in our environments, our brains will latch most easily on to the strongest signal. If that turns out not to fulfil its promise, our minds wander, looking for something new and more stimulating.

When you speak, you must maintain the level of interest above that of competing claims for our attention. This means a more dynamic delivery that engages our attention, a compelling narrative that creates a comfortable groove that is easy for us to follow, periodic surprises that remind us why we want to keep listening and, most fundamental of all, content that will intrigue us, interest us and provoke our thinking.

In this chapter, we will explore how you can gather interesting ideas and form them into narratives and opinions that people will want to hear.

You need to have something to say

Everybody has something to say. In fact we all have so much to say that the amount of information available is growing like nothing else, doubling almost yearly. The Library of Congress houses more than 150 million items, on 1,340km of shelves, growing at a rate of 10,000 items per day. But that is nothing: if the vast amounts of electronic data that we produce were created in printed form, we would need hundreds of billions of kilometres of shelves. To give you an idea of how big this is, Pluto is around 6 billion kilometres from the Sun.

So, if you want to find something interesting to say, you have an awful lot of competition. But, on the bright side, there is also a fantastic amount of material to learn from, build new connections between and draw upon for insights.

... but it doesn't have to be new

If you want me to listen to you, you don't have to find something new to say; you just need to find new and insightful ways to present some of this knowledge. Find ways to entertain and delight me, stimulate me and make me think, answer my questions and solve my problems. There is plenty of material for all of that.

An executive I coached wanted to build a story to help sales of the soft fruits his company imported. His potential clients are very familiar with all the measures of quality and industrial processes of bringing the fruit to market. But he wanted to entertain and delight his audience, so they would see his company's fruit in a different and positive way. So we got rid of all the usual material and started his presentation with a picture of a rose bush. He told his audience how many rose bushes their fruit growers had planted last year, and asked the question 'Why?' For his answer, he showed a beautiful picture of a bee and went on to explain how bees pollinate orange trees, but are attracted to rose bushes – so growers plant roses at the ends of rows of orange trees. The whole story of roses and bees allowed him to talk about the quality of his fruit and the growing practices in a way that was fresh, engaging and authentic.

Only with good material can you start to craft something interesting to say. So, before we look at how you can tell your story without waffling or being too abrupt, let's focus on where you can get your ideas from.

Be interested

To be interesting, you need to be interested. Curiosity is perhaps the greatest asset for anyone who wants to be interesting and speak about things that interest others.

→ **Be interested in people and what matters to them** – their passions and personalities, their triumphs and tragedies, their friends and families. This will make you a compelling person to be with – eager to hear other people's stories and able to recount interesting human tales.

→ **Be interested in events** – current affairs, the million daily events that shape society, the big movements in history, the small transformations that herald great changes. This will give you the source of commentary that will engage people's fascination for prediction.

→ **Be interested in ideas** – politics, philosophy, science, engineering, sociology, anthropology, psychology, design, art, music, drama, literature. Ideas give you interesting things to say and filters through which to view stories and events, allowing you to transform them into powerful insights that will grip people's imagination.

Being interested is recognising that everything is interesting if you examine it deeply. Everything is a source of valuable knowledge and ideas. What bores people is when we present interesting things in an unimaginative, monotonous way. So, with so much available to you, let's go out and find something interesting to talk about.

Meet people

The great source of information in society is society itself: the people who make it up. The more people you meet and take an interest in, the greater your store of ideas and stories.

Sadly, many of us find talking to people – especially new or unfamiliar people – a little intimidating. Yet it is new people who have most to offer you, so if you do find the thought of talking with people leaves you less than thrilled, it's time to master the art of chat.

The art of chat

Forget 'networking' and all the pressure that some career choices place on you to acquire a list of contacts you can call on for help, exploit for gain, or to whom you can sell. Instead, focus on the one skill that will not only give you lots of interesting things to speak about, but will also create real human contact that builds respect, liking and, eventually, friendship: chat.

Wherever you find yourself, take the opportunity to chat with others who are there too. Going places alone makes this much easier: going with a friend, relative or colleague means you are more likely to chat with them.

If you find the thought of going up to someone a little unsettling, think about how good you feel when someone comes up to you and breaks the ice by introducing themselves. They seem to be in control, confident and at ease. The chances are that they aren't: they probably just decided to go for it. If you do that and introduce yourself to me, it will be you who will come across as confident and in control. I will respond warmly, out of relief from feeling isolated in the group.

Speaker's tip: opening gambits

When you enter a room full of people you barely know, pick someone at the far end who is on their own. Now, stand up straight and walk slowly and purposefully towards them, acknowledging anyone you pass, whom you have met before, with a polite smile, nod of your head, and 'Hello'. When you get to them, make them feel special and introduce yourself at the same time, with 'Hello, I couldn't help noticing you, I am ...' Ideally, pick something flattering to notice. Better yet, before you approach them, find out who they are: 'Hello, Jamie, I've been hoping to speak with you. I am ...'

If these approaches don't seem appropriate, one opening gambit will always work: where you are. Either comment on where you both are, or ask them for their thoughts about it. This works because it is instantly something you have in common and creates immediate rapport.

When striking up a conversation, here are some useful tips:

Have an interesting way to describe yourself

Think about what would make the things you do interesting to other people. Hopefully you find your own life interesting, but why should I? Adapt your description to the person who is asking 'What do you do?' If you are in business to sell, then avoid the temptation to do it now. Instead, create intrigue about what you do. Instead of 'I sell luxury shoes' (dull), how about 'I help people look forward to a long day on their feet'?

When you meet people, ask questions, take an interest

This is, after all, what you are here for. But it is also the best way to strike up a rapport and build a relationship. Encourage conversation with statements and open questions such as 'Tell me about yourself' or 'What interests you most at the moment?' Then use more focused questions to learn more about what interests you in what they have said. They will be flattered when you probe for more detail, and will willingly supply it. Questions give you control of the process and are respectful of the other person.

We will come back to the topic of questioning and listening in Chapter 7, where we will focus on conversations.

The most interesting thing to me is ... me

So, if you ask me about myself, I will think your conversation is great. Here is your chance to learn about my experiences, so you can pick up stories and anecdotes; my opinions, so you can test, measure and adjust yours; and my expertise, so you can build your bank of knowledge. You never know when a snippet picked up today will be relevant and enhance your conversation or speech.

Let informal chat become worthwhile conversation

As you move from shallow chat to more substantial exchange of information, the techniques of conversation will start to take over, and the central technique is spotting and using **conversational hooks**.

When I speak or answer a question I will usually give a little bit more information than you asked me for. That extra snippet gives you a hook on to which you can hang another question, to open out the conversation.

'You're back from a business trip? Where did you go?'

'I went to Malta, it was a fascinating place.'

'Really; what did you find fascinating?'

You can use these hooks immediately, or come back to them later in your conversation. That way, you also show me you were listening to me; which is a great compliment and will certainly lead me to think a little better of you for it.

What if the hook doesn't come?

Some people don't like to talk a lot and will answer even the most open questions with short answers, offering no hook to another question.

If you keep asking questions, it will feel to both of you as if you are conducting an interrogation, rather than a conversation. So vary your approach, like this:

'Where was the factory you went to inspect?'

'Malta.'

'I've not been there; what did you think of it?'

'Interesting'

'Oh, interesting in what way?'

This is a **stretch question** that tries to stretch out a terse answer. To make it work, you have to avoid any sense of inquisition, so use body language that invites a response: lean in gently, turn one or both palms uppermost, and look them in the eye to show real interest. Stretch out the last syllable of your stretch question to emphasise that it is a genuine question, then gently lean back to relax into the answer. Usually, a couple of these stretch questions will open up a reticent conversationalist.

Preparing for a conversation

You will sometimes have the opportunity to prepare for a conversation in advance. You may be meeting local people you have heard about, business people you want to work with, or your partner's colleagues, whom you want to get on with. If you can, prepare beforehand.

Ask questions of colleagues or look them up, to find out what you can about them and their interests. Also find out what you can about their organisation, what it does and the jargon and hot topics that are commonplace in their industry.

This is easier to do now than it has ever been. Read their website or blog if they have one, their organisation's website, any industry or trade association websites, blogs, trade magazines, leaflets and social media. This last offers huge amounts of information about people. In the business context, it is wisest to stick to business social media websites such as LinkedIn or Plaxo, or deliberate channels like About.me or VisualCV. If you refer to information that can only be gathered from social websites, such as Facebook, that may be taken as intrusive.

Speaker's tip: sharing jargon

When we share a set of jargon or slang terms (known as an 'argot' by linguists) with other members of a group, we become a part of that group – as long as we do so properly. Researching and listening for the meanings and usages of argot words, and then using them appropriately can help you to build rapport and be accepted.

When you are with new people, listen for words and phrases they use that are unusual. Ask about them and, when you fully understand, start to use them and watch for reactions. Before meeting potential business partners, clients or funders, familiarise yourself as much as you can with their argot. It will help you communicate more effectively.

Be well informed

Never arrive anywhere without checking out some snippet of news that you can share. Better still; keep up to date with all the important news stories, so that you can discuss them. Particular settings will dictate the types of news that people will be interested to talk about: at the local sports club, people will be interested in the news from the current cricket tour, golf tournament or athletics meet. At town council meetings, politics and the contents of the local newspaper will come to the fore. Among friends, it may be the big stories of the day, the latest breakthrough in medical research, or today's celebrity gossip. When you are in a business context, it is absolutely vital that you are up-to-date with the latest news in your industry, so make trade and professional press a priority and find one or two good blogs or websites to scan regularly. Often you can subscribe to have news items delivered to your email inbox daily or weekly.

New ideas

Make time to look for novel ideas that will stimulate creative thinking and generate things for you to speak about and different perspectives on your usual topics. There are lots of places to look.

Speaker's checklist: ten great sources of ideas and inspiration

1 **Newspapers** – especially the features. Keep an eye on the business or policy sections that deal with your industry sector in all the quality newspapers.

2 **Magazines** – to stay informed, read professional and trade journals, and for stimulus try buying a new, randomly chosen magazine each month.

3 **Blogs** – don't just pick blogs about your professional and personal interests; read random blogs. You can find examples from a wide variety of topics at: **www.typepad.com**, **http://blogsofnote.blogspot.co.uk** or **http://wordpress.com**

4 **TV current affairs and documentary programmes** are often relevant to business issues. Keep an eye on what is coming up and look for connections to what your organisation does. If something is coming up that has direct relevance, record it so you can go back to it if it has a lot of detail you want to grasp.

5 **Drama** – good drama on TV, in movies and at the theatre is a constant source of ideas, new perspectives and, inevitably, stories. Most will seem irrelevant to a business context, but some will resonate strongly.

6 **Seminars, conferences and training courses** – treat them not as magic bullets to solve all your problems, but instead mine them for a few real nuggets that you can apply to your work.

7 **Exhibitions, galleries and museums** – these can give you great ideas about how to communicate ideas at work, as well as things to talk about. Many exhibitions are sponsored and may have direct relevance to your industry; seek these ones out.

8 **Information boards and plaques** that you can spot as you walk around town – these give you interesting asides, but also place your organisation in a solid context that you can use in marketing and selling conversations.

9 **Display boards** at libraries, municipal buildings, hospitals and schools – keeping an eye open wherever you go can deliver a host of unexpected yet useful ideas and insights. Sometimes you can spot genuine commercial opportunities here.

▶

10 **Leaflets, booklets and brochures** from visitor attractions, libraries, museums and galleries, public buildings or businesses – these are all examples of communication that you can learn from, and the information they contain can be interesting too. As a project management trainer, I found a leaflet about The Milestone Society gave me an idea for how to help people understand a vital part of project management.

And a bonus source:

11 **Books** – fiction or non-fiction, serious or humorous, heavy or light. Books are filled with ideas, stories and insights. There are many books that any serious business person, manager or leader could gain a lot from. Ask colleagues for recommendations and try to read at least four new work-related books a year.

Develop depth

Over the longer term, it will pay you to develop depth of knowledge and understanding in the topics that interest you most. This will enable you not only to pepper your conversation with interesting titbits, but to show real authority when you speak. As much as people love a tasty morsel here and there, they also crave a nourishing fulfilling feast. Make your learning meet both needs.

Shape your point of view

Being well informed is an entry-level requirement. For people to really hang on what you are saying you need a point of view on things that matter. It must be well informed, consistent and soundly structured. A strong point of view comes when you are able to create new insight for your audience.

When you can create greater understanding or new insights for your audience, they will want to listen. Here are seven ways that you can do this:

1 Drawing distinctions that are new.

2 Highlighting unexpected relationships.

3 Extending from 'what we all know' to what we can conclude or predict.

4 Linking 'what we all know' to something else we know.

5 Linking some new information to 'what we all know'.

6 Finding unexpected relevance in 'what we all know'.

7 Showing how new information has relevance to our current situation.

Moments of insight

Learning happens at that 'penny dropping' moment when you realise something you had never realised before and understand something you did not know before. Greater knowledge and understanding allows you to perceive how seemingly different things are related, or how seemingly similar things are, in fact, distinct.

A bat and a bird both have wings. Both fly and roost in trees. They are seemingly similar. When we realise that they are really very different and that these similarities are merely superficial, this is a **distinction insight**. As you become more expert, you make ever finer distinctions.

On the other hand, an eagle is a creature that flies with superb confidence, while a penguin has no wings – just flippers, like a sea lion. Both penguins and sea lions are wonderfully agile underwater. We understand nature better when we achieve a **relationship insight** and perceive how penguins and eagles are in fact similar. Experts have a deep understanding of how things relate to one another.

Moments of connection

We also learn by making connections. It's what our brains are supremely good at doing. So good, in fact, that we often make connections where none exist: bunny rabbits in the clouds; beasts among the stars. The connections that you make are of two types: either between two things you already know but were unaware of the connection; or between something you already know and something completely new.

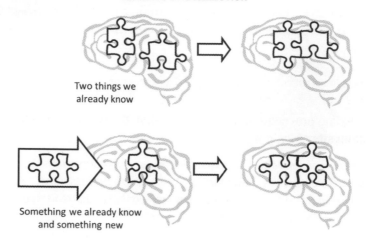

Two things we
already know

Something we already know
and something new

Model-building

One way to get people to listen is to present your ideas in a way that makes it easy for them to assimilate. Models are simplifications of the real world that retain the most important aspects, while dropping the peripheral, incidental details that have little impact on our comprehension. Once I understand your model, I can then build on that understanding as you add layers of subtlety and complexity.

In the language of mental filters that we explored in Chapter 2, you are helping me form a story that is a simplified representation of the real world, and then showing me how to put more detail on the various parts of it.

Three types of model

All models have descriptive power. However, some are better at describing different things. The three principal purposes of models are:

1 **Explanation:** Models that help us understand 'what is'.
2 **Prediction:** Models that help us predict what 'will be'.
3 **Process:** Models that help us achieve a reliable outcome.

Of course, some models achieve two or even all three of these in differing amounts. Shaping your understanding into a model can help your audience to understand, predict and achieve – all of which are compelling objectives.

As you read this book, you will find a large number of models – you have encountered several already, and we are only on page 31!

Creating provocation, pressure, tension, danger, excitement or mystery

Another reason why people will listen to you is if your opinions or ideas can create an 'edge of the seat' sensation. Now they just have to hear what comes next, because they want to hear how your provocation or complication can be resolved.

The way that you can do this is with the powerful question: **'what if?'** Now, your 'what if?' question is connecting 'what we know' with a scenario.

→ If the scenario contradicts 'what we know', then the 'what if?' creates a provocation.

→ If the scenario is a change, then the 'what if?' creates tension.

→ If the scenario is a need, then the 'what if?' creates pressure.

→ If the scenario is threatening, then the 'what if?' creates danger.

→ If the scenario is enticing, then the 'what if?' creates excitement.

→ If the scenario is unknown, then the 'what if?' creates a mystery.

Crafting your point of view

People want to hear something distinctive, a point of view. But it must be well informed and well crafted to be compelling and persuasive. So invest time in crafting your point of view on subjects that really matter to you.

Your point of view may be provocative, challenging received wisdom; or it may simply be a clear-minded assessment of the situation.

Speaker's tip: crafting your point of view

Here are the four components of a point of view. Think about each of these and write down your response clearly and succinctly. As part of the exercise, review the evidence that supports parts 1 to 3, so that you can defend your point of view if you are challenged. If this evidence is sound, then your invitation at part 4 will stand on its own merits.

Part 1: Observation – start with an observation that interests you, is salient to your overall message, and which either your audience will recognise immediately or you could demonstrate quickly.

Part 2: Understanding – what understanding can you bring to bear that will allow your audience to perceive the situation in a new way? This is your distinctive insight.

Part 3: Assertion – what does your observation mean? Make this as provocative as you choose, employing the 'what if?' technique to show the consequences.

Part 4: Invitation – this can be your call to action or a statement of what you propose to do, inviting your audience to support you.

The YES/NO of getting something to say

YES

→ Take an interest in other people and in all the events and ideas around you.

→ Vary your habits – reading, TV, cultural, etc. – to expose yourself to a wide range of ideas and influences.

→ Find a way to describe yourself that will interest other people.

→ Prepare for conversations when you can.

→ Make yourself well informed.

→ Shape a distinctive point of view.

NO

→ Don't be intimidated by new people. They have interesting stories and want to tell them.

→ Remember that nothing is boring if presented with passion, insight and clarity.

→ Don't consider any topic to be lacking in something of interest and value.

→ Don't bother with a 'me too' opinion that is just the same as everyone else's. Find your distinctive perspective.

Get attention

Chapter Four

Before you even open your mouth, people will start to decide whether they want to listen to you and how much they really want to hear. So how can you grab attention in a positive way and predispose people to want to listen to what you have to say? And once you start to speak, what are the ways that you can hold attention and sharpen people's desire to hear your message?

Getting attention is not about showy, vivid displays, but about making your presence known in a calm, dignified manner that announces 'I am here, and I am worth your attention'. To do this, you will need to master three stages:

1 **Your entry** – how you come into a room or on to a stage.

2 **Your presence** – your bearing; how you present yourself to people.

3 **Your hook** – how you grab the attention of your audience: whether one person, some people, or many.

And once you start to speak, you will also want to hold the attention you have worked to create, and sharpen people's desire to hear your message. So there is a fourth stage:

4 **Your hold** – how you maintain interest and therefore attention in what you are saying, right at the start, before you are warmed up with your content.

Make an entry

Your entry starts before you get to the threshold of the room or the steps of your platform. It needs physical and mental preparation.

Physical preparation

If you do your physical preparation well, it will have a profound effect on your confidence, so this is where you really 'psyche yourself up' – not with your mental preparation. You must get the basics right, so before you go on stage, enter a conference room full of people or even go into a key meeting with one or several people, pop into the cloakroom to check your physical appearance.

Of course, you may need to make yourself comfortable anyway, but a few moments of preening will give you a chance to calm your mind while focusing on something concrete. I suggest you create a ritual for yourself to ensure you check everything that matters: hair, teeth, make-up, jewellery and the look and line of your clothes for a woman, and, similarly, hair, teeth, tie or shirt-top, flies and the line of your clothes for men. Many people also find that washing and drying their hands (carefully, to avoid splashing your clothes) will help calm them.

The biggest impact, however, on the way you will feel and come across is created by the balance of stress and dominance hormones in your body. When you feel anxious, your cortisol levels rise in response to stress, and your testosterone levels drop. What if you could create a sense of confidence and power that caused a surge in testosterone levels and a dip in cortisol – whether you are a man or a woman?

From the laboratory: power posing to boost confidence and performance

We, like other animals, express our dominance and power through posture. Open, expansive postures (like hands on hips, legs somewhat apart) signify power, while closed postures (such as hunching, hugging, and crossing arms and legs) portray powerlessness.

Dana Carney and Andy Yap of Columbia University and Amy Cuddy of Harvard University investigated whether adopting these postures can affect our behaviours and social power. Their results were clear: adopting two high-power poses for just one minute each raised testosterone and decreased cortisol levels, increased feelings of power, and heightened tolerance for risk, in both men and in women. Low-power poses, typical of shy and retiring behaviours, had the opposite effect.

The impact on behaviour is so marked that adopting powerful or powerless poses before a mock job interview, carried out by a neutral interviewer, led four neutral observers to consistently award the jobs and assess the higher levels of performance to the power-posers. This, despite the fact that analysis of transcripts showed the answers were no better in content nor in structure. The confidence of delivery made all the difference.

Amy Cuddy presents her research in an entertaining video at **http://bit.ly/ TED-AmyCuddy**

Get attention

So try popping somewhere private for two minutes before going on stage, into your meeting or into your social event, and striking a **power pose**.

POWER POSES

Mental preparation

It is also important to prepare mentally: to remind yourself of what you most want to achieve in your speech, presentation, meeting contribution or conversation. If you have prepared well in advance then you have invested a lot of time, so now is your chance to harvest that investment. Rehearse one more time what you plan to do or say as an opener, and trust that your preparation and instincts will carry you forward.

Entering a room

You've done your power pose; now it's time for your **power pause**. Don't just enter the room: stop at the threshold. Make a power pause – take time to scan the whole room slowly and deliberately before stepping in. As you do so, you are not showing off in a 'look, I'm here' way, you are assessing what's going on in an 'I'm looking at you' sort of a way. Don't just look: listen too. Absorb the mood and patterns in the room: who is on their own; what groupings are there; which groups are open and which are closed, absorbed in their own discussions?

How to Speak so People Listen

Now select where you want to go first and then take a deep breath. Now, keeping your head high, arms loose and a smile on your face, set off confidently. Acknowledge people warmly on your way, as if to say 'Hello, old friend; I'm glad you've come'.

Working a room

The secret to working a room is to be aware of everyone in it, and the social groupings, and to use that knowledge to get around a representative sample. You need to take enough time with each person or group to demonstrate you are truly interested in them, but move on quickly enough to leave them wanting more. Here are the five key skills to cultivate.

1 Contact-making

2 Hand-shaking

3 Ice-breaking

4 Turn-taking

5 Attention-raking

Contact-making

The easiest people to approach are people on their own; they will be glad of the company. If you have a choice, start with people you think you would be most comfortable speaking with: people like you – the same gender and age, with similar dress sense.

If you want to speak with a pair or a threesome, look at the body language. If the pair is facing one another, they will probably not welcome a third. If, however, they are standing at an angle, the open space indicates willingness for someone to join them. It is the same with a threesome: an open space indicates 'open to new participants', while a tight triangle says 'keep out'. A group of four or more is harder to join.

Use your eyes to make first contact. For a singleton, look them in the eye and smile: contact is made. With a group, pick one person and do the same, but then wait to be invited into the group, to participate. Look interested and engaged, and start to echo the body language.

Hand-shaking

Once you have made contact, shake hands using the web-to-web technique, placing your whole hand to theirs, so that the webs between thumbs and forefingers meet. Keep your hand in the vertical plane, to signify equality: as soon as your hand turns slightly palm-down, you are signalling dominance and, likewise, with your palm slightly uppermost, you are being subtly submissive. Smile and keep eye-contact as you shake hands. Introduce yourself, saying your name slowly and clearly, and make a point of noting the other person's name, repeating it out loud: 'Chris, it's good to meet you.'

HAND-SHAKING

Even handshake   Dominating handshake

Ice-breaking

If you are joining a group, there will be a conversation to participate in, but with an individual you will need to start one. Keep it simple. The easiest approach is to comment on the event, the venue, the hospitality or the programme. Avoid commenting adversely, in case this is the person who designed the programme or recommended the caterer. Steer clear at the start of commenting on fellow participants, it's too risky. Safe topics to ask about include their journey, what attracted them to the event or if they know anyone else present.

Turn-taking

At a conference or meeting, you want to meet a representative group of people to make the biggest impression and also to give you exposure to the most new contacts and ideas. So, after five to ten minutes, it is time to move on. Here are a few great strategies.

Speaker's checklist: six strategies to move on from one conversation to a new one

→ 'I'm off to get a drink, would you care to join me?' They will probably decline, but if they do join you, they may introduce you to someone new.

→ 'May I introduce you to someone I met earlier?'... and leave them with them. This does them a favour, saving them from having to approach someone, and allows you to find someone else to talk with.

→ 'Did you mention you know Janice Davy? I wonder if you'd introduce me.' A great way to start a new conversation is with an implied endorsement.

→ 'Shall we separate and mingle?' This way you suggest that they too will have the confidence to move on.

→ 'I've monopolised you for too long, I hope we'll catch up later.' This implies a selfless reason for letting them go.

→ 'I'd like to continue this when we have more time; do you have a card?' This implies you are genuinely interested, but you must now follow up or risk looking disrespectful.

Attention-raking

How can you attract people to come and speak with you while you are already speaking with another person or group? The first step is to ensure that your pair or group is open, with space for someone to approach. It is also best to avoid holding a drink or, worse still, a plate. This reduces your ability to stand with an open, welcoming posture.

You will also gather more attention if you take up a position towards the centre of a room or at some focal point. Now, by standing with your open posture, you are saying 'Come to me, you're very welcome'.

Mounting a stage

Getting on stage or mounting a platform before speaking to an audience is a case of 'the same, but more so'. Come to the front of the stage confidently, looking as though you are entirely comfortable. Take your time and, when you arrive, survey your audience before starting. Wait until they settle down and become quiet, otherwise you will have to compete with the audience's noise – many will not be listening. If you wait, on the other hand, you are demonstrating your belief that you have something worthwhile to say.

If there is a host, walk straight to them and greet them like an old friend – even if you met for the first time ten minutes earlier. Shake their hand, and exchange a few words before turning to your audience. Stand still while they introduce you, smiling pleasantly and scanning the audience with your eyes, as if to say to each person 'I am looking forward to speaking to you'.

'All the world's a stage'

The need to make an immediate positive impact applies equally to approaching someone in your office, factory or warehouse, in a corridor, lift or lobby, or in the street, station or airport. What does it take to get somebody to pay attention to you? I mean to really pay attention, rather than just acknowledge you and rush off?

This matters because in modern organisational life five minutes in a corridor with your boss is sometimes all you are going to get this week. And if you need to influence her, or get an answer from him, or secure permission to do something, you are going to want to get all of their attention right away.

The sections that follow apply equally to these situations and to more formal meetings or presentations. And it is also equally true that you need to prepare: leaving the outcome of a 'chance meeting' to chance is amateurish. Plan what you want to say, how you are going to say it, and what your opening line will be to grab attention.

If you are going to go to that much trouble – and if it matters, you should – then you may as well go to the trouble of engineering your chance meeting too. I don't mean stalk and pounce, but find out when you will get opportunities to run into the potential client, senior executive or politician you want to speak with and choose a moment where they are most likely to be receptive: not in a hurry, not preoccupied with another matter, and not with someone else. Set up the situation in your favour.

Have presence

'Presence' is a pretty difficult concept to define. Dictionaries speak of an imposing or dignified bearing. In another context, they add: 'an invisible spirit, felt nearby'. It is certainly something we recognise in some people, but not in others.

To me, the secret of presence ... is all about being present. One hundred per cent here, in the moment. This means using your power pause before speaking – especially to an audience – to become present in the moment and take in everything and everyone around you. The more you absorb their presence, the more of a commanding presence you become. When you are in a smaller meeting, or speaking one-to-one, the rule has to be: *When you are in the room; be in the room.*

This means not letting your mind wander. Give *all* your attention to the person or people you are speaking with.

Positively relaxed

Posture seems to be a big part of presence. Appearing relaxed and energetic at the same time creates a powerful impression of calm control. It starts with releasing unwanted tension in your back, shoulders and neck, which, by the way, can also be the cause of chronic back pain. Let's try a three-step technique.

1 Release
2 Breathe
3 Project

Release

Become aware of how your neck and shoulders feel. If you cannot easily just release the tension that is there and relax, instead try hunching your shoulders and tensing your neck for a moment. Then release. Repeat that exercise twice more and you will start to get a feel for the difference. Another place we often carry tension is in our jaw, so wiggle your jaw, stretch and move your tongue and exercise your lips, to release tension there. Now work down your body, feeling for unnecessary muscle tension, and letting it go. If you can't feel any, try the clench and release approach.

Now stand tall. Imagine you are a puppet with a string attached to the top of your head. Let that string pull you up to your full height, until you are nice and light on your feet. If that string is taking some of your weight, you should be able to move effortlessly. Whenever you enter a room or step on stage, picture that string lifting you upright, into a good posture and giving you a light feeling. Pick it up at the door when you go into the room. Let it lift you out of your chair as you get up to go on stage. Allow it to help you glide easily from the edge of the stage to your commanding position at the front.

BAD POSTURE / GOOD POSTURE

Bad posture   Good posture

Breathe

To maintain your positive relaxation you must, of course, keep breathing. As you get nervous, your breathing becomes shallow, working from your upper chest. This not only creates a feedback loop, sending anxiety signals back to your brain, but your pattern of breathing is visible to your audience, who can read it subconsciously. They will sense your anxiety.

So take control of your breathing and breathe down into your tummy. A few deep breaths – drawing in a large volume of air as far down as you can, to a count of five, followed by a slow exhale to a count of five – will steady your nerves and calm you, as well as replenishing your blood's oxygen supply. Try breathing in through your nose and out through your mouth.

How to Speak so People Listen

Project

Now you are relaxed and breathing, the third stage of positive relaxation is to project your energy outwards, to your listener or audience. Imagine there is a bubble around you, centred right inside your tummy, just below your navel. Imagine it expanding outwards to reach each person you are speaking to, whether one individual or a whole audience. Imagine that bubble is exerting a pressure outwards on your listeners. If you are speaking publicly, to a large audience, imagine that bubble expanding to fill the whole room, auditorium or stadium. That is your power, your presence … your charisma.

Speaker's toolkit: body language

An understanding of body language is an essential component of any speaker's toolkit. It is a whole discipline in itself and you will find some useful books in the 'Learn more' appendix. Here are a few simple tips – not intended as a guide, more as a stimulus to further research.

Open and symmetrical

Open and symmetrical postures – whether standing or seated – convey confidence and honesty. This doesn't mean the speaker isn't faking it, but that is how we read bodies. On the other hand, closed up postures – crossed arms and legs, and hunched shoulders – convey weakness and a lack of confidence. Asymmetric postures can give the impression of confusion at best, dissembling at worst.

Hand movements

Your hands can either emphasise the message of your words, or detract from them. Natural and expansive gestures have most impact and emphasise big ideas and ambitious statements. Small gestures support intimate confidences.
One of my own top tips is when counting off with your hands, or marking a direction of travel in the air, practise getting the direction right for your audience. If you grew up in the West, where we think of things moving from left to right through time, practise gesturing from your right to your left to indicate movement from past to future. That way, your audience will see a left to right movement. ▶

Facial expressions

An expressive face allows people to warm to you and gives them a shortcut to understanding the emotional messages you want to convey. As elsewhere, your expressions need to match your message. Any mismatch will be interpreted adversely and your message will be lost.

Fidgets and give-aways

The best tip is *don't*. Keep control of your hands: don't scratch, stroke or fiddle. Each gesture has a host of interpretations, both accurate and nonsense. But you don't want people interpreting what you are doing with your pencil or why you are scratching your nose. You want them to listen to you. Put your pen down, leave your hair alone, let your nose itch.

Dressed to thrill

How you dress has an important role to play in your presence. Your clothes and appearance need to strengthen your presence rather than detract from it. Choose clothes that are authentic to you – but not at the cost of isolating you from the people you want to listen to you. If in doubt, dress well, ensuring you are as smart as the people around you and, ideally, one notch smarter.

It is said that 'people like people who are like they want to be'. By dressing for the role that your audience or conversational partner aspires to, you will impress and influence them subtly.

You can make a big impact with simple choices when you pay attention to the details:

→ Your clothes must fit perfectly.

→ Make sure your clothes look immaculate – dandruff and unwanted creases can be your worst enemy.

→ Emphasise high-quality accessories: belts, brooches, ties. These can draw the eye, without distracting: a low-cost way to make you look stunning.

→ Take good care of your footwear. Not everyone will notice it but, for those who do, it speaks volumes.

The eyes have it

Your eye-contact tells me that you are interested in me, it holds my attention and compels me to listen to you. When speaking with one person, or a small group, deep, intense eye-contact with someone else who is speaking tells them that you value their words. When you speak, holding eye-contact not only keeps people focused on you, it also signals that you mean what you are saying.

With a larger audience, rather than just scanning across the whole room, stop and hold one person in your eye for the duration of a sentence or key clause in what you are saying. Then move to someone else. For a moment, that person will believe you are talking directly to them and it will have a huge impact on them.

For some people eye-contact is uncomfortable. If you are one of them, practise it. Each time, try to hold contact for a little longer. It may never feel wholly natural to you, but you will become more sensitive to what is right for the other person.

Knowing when to break eye-contact is just as important as being able to maintain it. Luckily, there are ample clues, if you allow yourself to be sensitive to them. Our eyes are forever making tiny darting movements across the face we are looking at, even when we think we are looking someone in the eye. This is true of the person you are looking at, too. The movements are called saccades. If the person starts to become uncomfortable with your eye-contact, the frequency and duration of their saccades, away from your eyes, will increase. You can sense this unconsciously. Now is the time to break eye-contact – just before they feel forced to.

Speaker's checklist: how to be likeable

Good eye-contact is one of the things that make us more likeable. Here are six more:

→ **Smiling** – naturally and easily, involving lots of facial muscles: a 'Duchenne' smile, rather than a 'mouth-only' fake smile.

→ **Familiarity** – unless you do something to antagonise me, the more familiar you seem, the more I will like you. Get to know people.

▶

→ **Compliments** – sincerely meant and openly expressed: not to be confused with false flattery, which I will spot. A great way to do this is to compliment me when you speak to someone else. When I hear about this (or even overhear it), I will be delighted.

→ **Interest** – take a genuine interest in me and whatever I find interesting: ask good questions and listen to the answers.

→ **Openness** – an air of mystery may intrigue me, but if you want me to like you, I need to feel you are open with me.

→ **Enthusiasm** – show enthusiasm for the things I do or say: 'Good point', 'Nice work', 'Well done', 'Fantastic!' or 'Thank you' have a big impact.

Simply you

Don't try to be someone you are not. It's a lie and you will be spotted. This is not the same as the 'fake it 'til you make it' approach – acting 'as if' you are already the 'you' that you want to be. Let's distinguish the two:

→ **Acting 'as if'** is authentic, because you are allowing the inner you to show itself, perhaps before you feel as if you have wholly earned the right to be that person.

→ **Trying to be someone else**, because you think that persona may be more valid, impressive or successful, is inauthentic, because it is not about showing the deeply buried inner you: it is about pretending to be what you are not and, more important, what you would never truly want to be.

As an alternative to 'fake it 'til you make it', perhaps we should say *'fake it while you become it'*.

Small changes make a big difference. React in ways that are honest to you, but control some of the outward manifestations of your behaviour, to give you a more powerful presence.

Speaker's checklist: charisma

When we put all this together, it takes us towards what is often called **charisma**. But I think that there is more to charisma. It is an ability to influence, inspire and enthuse, and needs more than just presence. Here are 12 further things to work on.

→ **Listening** – when you listen to me absolutely intently, shutting out all other distractions, it feels charismatic to me.

→ **Courage** – when you are capable of making the choices, taking the stances or doing the deeds that are right but not easy, that will seem charismatic.

→ **Discipline** – when you keep going through adversity, pain or pure tedium, because something really matters, that is character and charisma.

→ **Confidence** – when you refuse to be intimidated by uncomfortable situations, differing points of view or challenges to your authority, I feel your charisma.

→ **Spontaneous** – when you can respond quickly and authentically to changes in circumstances, you are demonstrating your charisma.

→ **Measured** – when your spontaneity consistently produces a measured, appropriate and effective response, your charisma gains authority.

→ **Risk-taking** – when your measured response allows calculated risk-taking, rather than always playing it safe, that seems charismatic.

→ **Visionary** – when you can see what others do not, spot trends, discern meanings and seize opportunities, that is charismatic.

→ **Expressiveness** – when you are able to control your emotions and to express them appropriately, so that people can see the authentic you, that is charismatic.

→ **Passion** – when you are enthusiastic and obviously care, and are steered by a value-set you truly hold, whether I agree or not, that is charismatic.

→ **Fluency** – when you can put your case articulately and eloquently, making a compelling, persuasive and powerful case, your speech becomes charismatic.

→ **Responsiveness** – when you are responsive to other people, to their demeanour, their needs and their desires, they will value your charismatic presence.

Hook your audience

When you are speaking to someone, or to an audience, they will almost certainly give you the benefit of the doubt and listen attentively for a short while. But attention quickly wanders if we are not hooked by what we are hearing, so you need to deploy your hook as quickly as possible. Your hook will answer your listener's inner question: 'If I listen, what's in it for me?'

Whether trying to hook an audience of one, some or many, marketers and advertisers have a simple formula for hooking their audience. They call it AIDA. AIDA is a four-stage hook that you can use any time.

Speaker's toolkit: AIDA

Stage 1: Attention

Grab your listeners' attention with something surprising, shocking, curious, or absolutely relevant to their experience.

Stage 2: Interest

Pique their interest by showing how it can benefit them. Note that attention and interest are focused on what your audience wants, not what you can offer.

Stage 3: Desire

Now create a real desire by showing what they will get if they listen to you. Show how what you can offer can fulfil your audience's desires.

Stage 4: Action

Let them know what they need to do next to get what they want.

You can use AIDA as the structure for an entire talk, using 'attention' and 'interest' to introduce it, or as a simple way to introduce a topic.

Attention grabbers

There are many things that can grab the attention of a listener or audience. Here are some, roughly in order of increasing impact. Notice how, as you start the list, you want to read down further, to find out what is coming. It is the 'keep the best for last' ploy.

Speaker's checklist: attention grabbers

→ Necessary responsibility

→ Agenda laid out

→ Relevant insight

→ Bizarre fact

→ Surprising insight

→ Shocking revelation

→ Pressure relieved

→ Advice requested

→ Guilt assuaged

→ Pain alleviated

→ Conscience pricked

→ Promise made

→ Fulfilment teased

→ Secret shared

→ Secret withheld

→ Problem solved

→ Mystery established

Setting up their memory

In Chapter 2, we identified six levels of speaking (page 12). The fifth was 'How to speak so people remember what you want them to'.

When you are speaking formally, to an audience, you should also aim to start to create the conditions for memory as early as possible. A neat little tool to help you with this is **the speaker's filing cabinet**.

Speaker's toolkit: the speaker's filing cabinet

Set up the context

We each have hundreds of mental filing cabinets, for the many different areas of our lives and the interests we have. Your audience needs to know which mental filing cabinet your information relates to.

Spell out your aim

What will your talk or presentation achieve? This enables your audience to create and label the right drawer in their mental filing cabinet.

Describe the benefits

All this will take energy: the mental energy to concentrate. Why should your audience bother? Here is where you answer their question: 'If I listen, what's in it for me?'

THE SPEAKER'S FILING CABINET

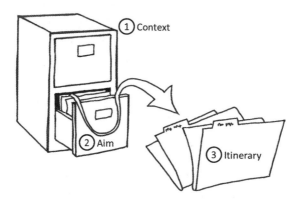

Map out your itinerary

Giving your audience a clear idea of the structure and sequence of your talk can allow them to mentally lay out all the folders that they will need, to file away the information you give them.

A handy mnemonic to help you remember this is CABInet: context, aim, benefits, itinerary.

Hold your audience

Holding your audience's attention, whether you are in an intimate one-to-one situation or on the platform in a vast conference auditorium, relies on four factors: freshness, directness, trust and rapport. We will tackle rapport in Chapter 7, so let's concentrate here, on the other three.

Freshness

We have all heard people speak whose words seem to flow as if from a thousand familiar scripts. All they seem to speak is clichéd and commonplace. **Management-speak** is a typical example of this. If you don't have anything original to say, then your conversation is nothing more than a pastime and your platform presentation is a waste of time: yours and your audience's. In meetings across the UK, thousands of hours are wasted everyday by people endlessly repeating what everyone around the table already knows. If that is all you have to say: shut up.

Instead, pick one specific area where you have depth of understanding and find something fresh to say. A new fact, a new interpretation or a new perspective. And find interesting, surprising ways to say things. Use language like an art-set with different pens, pencils, paints and crayons. Not only can language allow you to say an infinite number of things, but it also gives you the materials to say any of them in an infinite number of ways.

Directness

We get bored by circuitous, circumlocutory, roundabout and repetitious language. You see? Say what you mean, and say it as clearly as you can.

Above all, avoid euphemisms. These are words and phrases that help us avoid saying what we really mean for fear ... well, often for fear of being understood. How many times have you heard about downsizing, right-sizing, smart-sizing, out-placement, collateral damage, enhanced interrogation techniques, discrepant recommendations, terminological inexactitude?

But in your endeavour to be direct, you can still use interesting and colourful language, such as metaphors and analogies, which make your point clearly in an interesting and entertaining way. Above all, however, keep coarse language for the street or for theatre scripts.

Trust

We earn long-term trust through integrity. So how can we apply that knowledge to earning trust as we speak? This is taking us towards one of the three secrets of persuasive argument that we will discover in the next chapter: **ethos**.

To build trust, you first need to show that there is no reason to distrust you: you must show you have no inappropriate interest and declare any interest that you do have. That said, you must be able to demonstrate that you care about the topic and how it affects your audience: there is a limit to the distance disinterest should put between you and your audience.

You must also show that what you say is consistent with what you have actually done and that it is backed up by real experience and verifiable evidence. Add to that the need to demonstrate that your judgement is good and that the judgements you make are fair, and the trust test can sometimes be challenging.

This brings us back to something that came up earlier in the chapter, in the context of presence: the need to be authentic. If you speak from the heart, directed by your own ethical compass, then people will listen. They may not agree, but they will respect you and pay attention out of respect.

The YES/NO of getting attention

YES

→ Prepare before you make your entry.

→ As you enter, make excellent eye-contact, practise positive relaxation and use your power pauses.

→ Work the room.

→ Dress one notch up from the people you want to impress.

→ Practise the authentic you: 'fake it while you become it'.

→ Focus on what your audience is interested in hearing about.

→ Set your audience up to remember what you say with the speaker's filing cabinet – context, aim, benefits, itinerary.

→ Use fresh, direct and honest speech.

NO

→ Avoid slouching, scowling, fidgeting and fiddling.

→ Avoid sloppy dressing and grooming.

→ Don't be the phoney you: pretending to be someone you are not.

→ Don't use clichés and the same-old familiar ideas.

→ Avoid roundabout speaking and euphemisms that obscure the truth.

→ Never use inappropriate coarseness.

Get your message across

Chapter Five

Once you have attention, you need to use it to get your message across. How can you make your message compelling, persuasive and powerful? We will look at the way to structure and deliver your ideas so that people understand them easily, and how to make those ideas stick, paying special attention to what you can learn from the art of story-telling. We will examine the three components of a persuasive argument and how to harness the impact of words.

Compelling, persuasive and powerful

In Chapter 2, you met six levels of speaking.

THE SIX LEVELS OF SPEAKING

Compelling	Level 1. How to speak so people listen
	Level 2. How to speak so people understand
Persuasive	Level 3. How to speak so people understand, as you intend them to
	Level 4. How to speak so people agree with you
Powerful	Level 5. How to speak so people remember what you want them to
	Level 6. How to speak so people think or do what you want them to

You can address all these levels by making your speech compelling, persuasive and powerful. Let's examine what I mean by each of these three terms, and how they address our six levels.

Compelling

Compelling speech engages the listener and compels them to keep listening. It does so by adopting a structure that is simple and so clear that it makes it easy for us to follow, yet has enough surprise or interest to stop us getting bored.

Consequently, we want to hear more – addressing level 1 – and we understand it easily, addressing level 2.

We will see that there are a number of powerful ways to structure your speaking, and that we can also learn a lot about making our speech compelling from the great story-tellers of history.

Persuasive

The next requirement is that your speech must persuade your listeners to your point of view – or at least to accept that your perspective is reasonable and valid. Persuasive speech uses a range of tools to argue your case so that your audience will understand you as you intend them to. Your goal is for them to agree with you: they may not. At the very least, you want them to believe that what you say has integrity.

Persuasive speech addresses levels 3 and 4.

Speaker's toolkit: how to spot when an argument becomes a fight

The purpose of making an argument is to persuade: to achieve agreement. The purpose of two people arguing with one another is also for them to achieve agreement. For that to work, both parties need to listen, and to share a commitment to explore the evidence together. When you are speaking persuasively, your goal is to present the evidence in the most effective way to achieve that agreement. As soon as your goal becomes 'to win the argument', you have lost. Now you are fighting, because you are focusing on a binary choice: either you are right, or you are wrong. Life is rarely that simple.

It gets worse, too, because once we find ourselves fighting, winning can become just our first objective. When we win, we may then want to extract some form of reward or tribute, or we may even want to punish the other person.

As soon as you feel yourself wanting to win, take a mental step back and review your motives. People want to listen to an argument, but not get caught in a fight. And if they do start to fight, then you can be sure that they are no longer listening.

Powerful

Powerful speech works with our emotions and psychology to deliver your message in ways that change your audience: what they think, what they will remember and how they will act. When you speak with power, you have an impact on your listeners, and this addresses levels 5 and 6.

This chapter offers tools and techniques to make your speech compelling, persuasive and powerful. There is so much to say about creating an impact with powerful speech that we will return to the topic in the next chapter. Here, we will confine ourselves to the impact of words: your principle tools for getting your message across. In Chapter 6, we will tackle the techniques of influence, persuasion and memory.

Compelling: how to create a compelling and engaging structure

There are many different methods for creating a logical and compelling structure for you to follow in your speech. Some address the needs of formal speech, in front of an audience, and go back to the classical Greek and Roman orators. Others offer simple formulae to help you articulate an idea effectively in a meeting, a corridor or a café. We will also look at modern approaches to building effective presentations.

Finally, there is much we can learn from the art of the story-teller. Over the thousands of years of sitting around campfires, firesides, stages and televisions, lots of narrative structures have been created by bards, authors and dramatists that hook and hold audiences for hours on end.

We will look at some of the infinite variety of ways to structure what you say into a beginning, a middle and an end.

Oratory and the classical approach

The great Roman orators perfected the art of persuasive speech at the start of the Common Era, and their techniques were studied and documented in the Middle Ages.

GREAT ROMAN ORATOR

If we set aside the unfamiliar Latin terms, the structure they evolved was simple. You can still hear it in contemporary political speeches. It can also work for you. Its six steps are:

Step 1: Introduction

The introduction serves two functions: to hook your audience's interest and to demonstrate your character: why *you* are worth listening to.

Step 2: Narration

Keep this second step short and simple. Your only job is to tell the story, arranging the facts into a straightforward sequence that your audience will be able to follow easily. You don't want to shock, confuse or challenge them in any way; you are simply trying to ease them into your argument gently. Keeping things in chronological order often works best.

Step 3: Division

Now you can complicate matters with a contentious, surprising or shocking revelation, because here is where you set up the scope of the argument. This is why you need to speak. Set out where you agree with your audience or opponent and where you disagree – and why it matters. Is it about morality, values, beliefs, rights, fairness, interpretation, expediency or simply practicality?

Limit the number of essential points of disagreement so that you can focus on the big issues. If you try to make too many points you will come across as small-minded and obsessed by trivia. Three points is a good maximum.

Step 4: Proof

Now make your case. Present your evidence in a reasoned way, and demonstrate why you are right. The bases of proof, in order of reducing impact, are appeals to:

→ empirical evidence;
→ logical deduction;
→ rational thought;
→ common knowledge and practice.

Beware the last of these: many customs and social mores, which once seemed self-evidently, right now appear to us as just barmy. Which of our society's conventions will seem, to our children, to be equally absurd?

Step 5: Refutation

If you are arguing, your opponent will dispute your proof, so dilute the impact of their arguments by anticipating them. The more you can do to list and effectively counter all your opponent's objections and counterpoints, the weaker their arguments will seem when they make them. In sales, professionals use the term **emptying the hopper** to refer to drawing out and dealing with all your potential customer's objections. You should empty the hopper of your opponent's objections before they get a chance to make them. This also gives you the advantage to frame their points in a way that suits your argument.

Step 6: Conclusion

It is time to finish. This is where you restate your strongest arguments to reinforce memory ('tell them what you told them') and use an emotional message to hammer home the power of your points.

Speaker's toolkit: an example of the classical approach to a speech

Step 1: Introduction

Scientific innovation has created much of the world as we enjoy it today; solving problems in areas such as disease, communication, transport and agriculture. As a former professional scientist, new discoveries continue to fascinate me.

Step 2: Narration

Our development of space technologies has brought about a revolution in communication, transport, safety and our understanding of the universe.

Step 3: Division

Some people will tell you that, in a time of economic tension, we should reduce our investment in learning and the scientific exploration of space. We should certainly spend our money wisely, but I suggest two great and compelling reasons to exercise our curiosity about the universe around us.

First, we can never predict the tangible benefits that these programmes of research will bring us. And second, we can never underestimate the value to our society of learning, innovation and the excitement of discovery.

Step 4: Proof

Let us consider three examples. First, there is discovery of new materials, such as metal alloys used in medical implants that save lives. Second, consider the global positioning system (GPS) that allows easy and safe navigation anywhere in the world. And third, think of our ability to monitor and understand complex and violent weather systems, to better predict natural disasters. ▶

Step 5: Refutation

My opponents will tell you that we might have made these advances anyway. And we might. But would we have? Where is their evidence? They may say that we don't need the luxury of the knowledge that exploration brings us. But is it a luxury? Was it a luxury when explorers crossed the globe, when mankind learned the skill of writing, or when that skill became commonplace and not just the preserve of a few?

And my opponents will tell you we cannot afford this. But we can. It is simply a matter of priorities: we can afford warships and fighters and missiles and tanks. The question is: 'Can we afford not to?'

Step 6: Conclusion

Curiosity and self-interest: what more compelling reasons can we have to mount an endeavour? Perhaps one: the future of our children. Who knows what future fate holds for us? One thing only is certain: the more we know, the more we learn and the more we innovate, the more options we have to face the future with, and the more resources we have to solve whatever problems we face. We must keep up the pace of discovery, for the sake of the next generation.

Keeping it simple: structured response frameworks

One of the most useful skills for a speaker is to be able to quickly give a structured response to an argument or to an observation that will carry the authority of a prepared speech such as the one above, but without the need for preparation. You may, for example want to put a point at a meeting, to respond to something someone says to you in the lift, or create a compelling argument when your boss suggests something in the corridor.

While there would be nothing wrong with following the six steps of introduction, narration, division, proof, refutation and conclusion, you might find this tricky to remember, cumbersome to apply or too pompous for the situation. I know I do, so I have been collecting simpler frameworks to use for creating a structured response. Once you know one of these, you can simply follow the steps, inserting relevant information or observations to create a compelling argument that will sound polished and professional, with little or no preparation.

My favourites are below. Pick just one or two that you find compelling – either because the structure fits the situations you are likely to encounter, or because you find the mnemonic easy to memorise. Some are variants of each other.

Speaker's toolkit: structured response frameworks

Pain and pill

→ **Pain** – describe my problem and let me know you understand the pain I'm feeling.

→ **Pill** – offer your pill and let me know how you can help me.

Example: 'Our business is suffering because our competitors are getting deliveries to our customers more quickly. I have been examining some new delivery management services and believe we can cut our delivery time in half.'

BID

→ **Background** – summarise the situation and what is salient about it.

→ **Issues** – what is the problem and why does it matter?

→ **Decision** – describe what you will do (or would do) to address the issue.

Example: 'Since the winter, we have been left with a lot of excess stock in our warehouse. This is making it hard to manage goods inwards efficiently and has reduced our working capital. I propose we agree to sell off last season's stock at a big discount to free up space and generate cash.'

PEP

→ **Point** – make your point or state your position.

→ **Example** – illustrate your point with a compelling example.

→ **Point** – restate your position to reinforce it.

Example: 'We need to offer ABC Inc. a bigger discount. They have started to buy from our competitors even though our product is better, and last month we lost another contract, to supply their transport division. Now is the time to review our terms with ABC.'

▶

PRESS

→ **Point** – make your point or state your position.

→ **Reason** – explain why you take that position.

→ **Example** – illustrate your point with a compelling example.

→ **Summary** – summarise your argument or restate your position.

→ **Suggestion** – give a call to action about what you suggest we do.

Example: 'I want to arrange a sales trip to China to explore opportunities there. Sales are flat in our current markets, but China is a growing market we have not exploited. Now is the time to move into China. I recommend we allocate a budget to get us started and plan a trip for April, which is the ideal time.'

PPP

→ **Position** – explain the position we are in.

→ **Pressure** – describe the pressure that puts us under.

→ **Point of view** – give your perspective on this: what it means or how we should respond.

Example: 'The project is running four weeks late. This means we are at risk of losing all of next year's planned revenue from it. It is time to commit significant extra resources to getting it back on track.'

Hook, line and sinker

→ **Hook** – establish a need or appeal to an interest.

→ **Line** – provide a solution or a compelling offer.

→ **Sinker** – offer a convincer to show the offer or solution is sound.

Example: 'We need to replace our warehouse automation system before failure rates impact customer service. The XYZ system meets our needs precisely. If we commission by the end of next month, we can get an extra discount and get the work finished during our quiet period.'

CSI – a forensic analysis of the situation

→ **Context** – what's happening?

→ **Subtleties** – what details do you perceive that make it more complicated?

→ **Insight** – what does this tell you about what the events really mean?

Example: 'We have lost five good staff members in two months, to IJK Limited. When Mary left, she hinted that she would be working on an internet project. I think IJK are about to launch a web service that could steal a lot of our business.'

EIOU

→ **Event** – what has happened?

→ **Implications** – what does that mean for us?

→ **Options** – what are our choices?

→ **Urging** – which option do you recommend?

Example: 'The council has just granted planning consent for that new estate of 560 houses. With lots of new families, there will be new opportunities. We could expand our shop to sell more convenience items, or start a range of toys, gifts and fancy goods. I think we should go for the gifts, because the extra houses could attract a new supermarket.'

Building a presentation for a modern audience

The first advice that many business speakers get makes a lot of sense: 'Tell them what you are going to say, tell them it, and then tell them what you said.'

When expressed so bluntly, it sounds like a dull way to present, but it does fulfil some of the demands of compelling, persuasive and powerful speech. The introduction creates a mental map that addresses part of your speaker's filing cabinet (see Chapter 4) and the repetition will help with memory, as we will see in the next chapter.

But without more detail, this advice falls short of telling you how to hold attention, let alone persuade. So, more sophisticated approaches are needed, which set out how to structure an effective presentation of your ideas. These work by splitting your material into a beginning, a middle and an end, and showing you how to structure each of them.

What makes the process of developing a compelling, powerful and persuasive presentation more complicated is that it pays not to start at the beginning of your talk, but with the heart of it, your **central idea.**

The figure below illustrates the sequence that your presentation will follow. The numbers against each section indicate the order in which I recommend you develop your material.

A COMPELLING, PERSUASIVE AND POWERFUL PRESENTATION

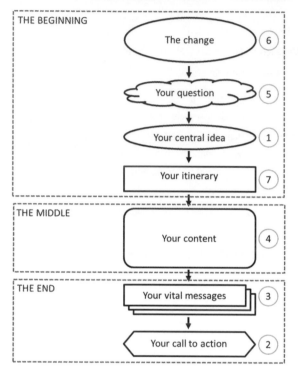

Let's now work through the steps in creating your compelling, persuasive and powerful presentation. We will follow the ideal order for creating it, rather than the order you will present it in.

The central idea

Your central idea is the heart of your formal presentation: the point of view that you want to communicate and persuade others of. This is your big thought and your **reason** for speaking. So it is the obvious place to start. The tools to help you find your idea are in Chapter 3. Contained within your central idea must be a sense of why it is important to your audience. Without a reason to listen, their unconscious minds will be asking 'Why?', distracting them from listening to you by trying to find the answer. Think about how you will convey your reason.

In journalistic jargon, this is your **lead**, and a journalist knows that this will dominate their first sentence. It contains all the most essential elements of their story and will be followed by more information in order of reducing importance: the 'inverted pyramid'. Losing the essence of the story or 'burying the lead' is a journalistic sin. This is true for you too, so this is why you must start by planning your talk around your central idea.

The end

Now hop to the very end of your presentation and think about what you want your audience to do as a result of your central idea – and why and how. This will give you your **call to action**. It sets up the difference that you want your speaking to make.

But the end section needs to serve two purposes: not just a call to action, but also a summary of your **vital messages**. The perfect number of messages is three. Choose your vital messages to clearly justify your call to action or to set your audience up with the knowledge they need to carry it out. In Chapter 6, we will concentrate on how to make these messages powerful.

The middle

Occupying the middle of your presentation – and probably taking the majority of your time, is your **content**. This is here for one reason only: to set up your vital messages.

Your content will fill out your central idea and make it real and tangible, by giving the answer to one of the three great questions: why, what or how.

→ **Justify:** The 'why' question demands that you justify your central idea with evidence and reasoning that make it believable. A typical sequence for your content would present your evidence, then its implications or the problems that arise, then your solution. You might want to introduce endorsements and testimonials, or demonstrations to provide supporting evidence.

- → **Explain:** The 'what' question requires you to explain your central idea in clear and easy terms that allow your audience to understand what your idea is and what its implications are, for them. When you explain your idea, your content might be of a 'this-not-that' structure or follow a set of categories. Make good use of metaphors and analogies to help you explain complex concepts, or, better still, use props or demonstrations so your audience feel they have a first-hand experience of your central idea.

- → **Demonstrate:** The 'how' question requests that you demonstrate how your central idea works, so that it becomes practical. Your content will therefore be likely to follow a sequence that sets out a process. If you can demonstrate that process, or a representative version of it, to your audience, then so much the better.

The beginning

You have your central idea, but where does it come from? It must be the answer to a question or a problem or a discomfort. This is your **question**. Your talk will be most powerful when this question, problem or discomfort is important to your audience right now.

Next, think about where your question comes from. Something must have triggered it and that is the **change**. Something must have changed, even if it was only your perception and that you simply became aware of something you had not noticed before. Either you have learned something new, or the world has actually changed in some way. Spell out how reality has changed: how the present situation differs from before. This is critical, because without change, there is no story … and stories engage us.

When you start your talk, start with 'the before'. Reality as we knew it did not seem threatening, so opening with this is comfortable for your audience. It puts them at their ease and helps you build rapport with them by directing their attention towards something 'we all know and share'.

But in 'the now', something has changed. That should unsettle your audience and heighten their awareness. Their concentration will increase, and may be even sharpened by a little adrenalin if the change is dangerous, suspenseful or confusing.

So now, when you ask your question, it should echo a question in your audience's minds. They should care about what the answer is and, indeed, will be seeking an answer for themselves. They will certainly be interested to hear how you will answer that question. Now, when you speak, they will listen. They are waiting for your answer; they are waiting for your central idea.

The last thing to work on is your **itinerary** – how you will describe what will come next. We saw why this is important in Chapter 4. Keep it simple and map out how you will present your content, so your audience knows what to expect and will be able to chart your progress as you go.

Sequencing your beginning

So, your beginning has five elements:

1 The before
2 The now
3 Your question
4 Your central idea
5 Your itinerary

Speaking is a little like playing jazz: once you know the rules, you can play around with them to create different effects. Sometimes you can drop one or more of your five elements. For example:

→ Drop your itinerary if your content is short, simple in structure, or follows a clear story arc.

→ Drop your before if your now is already commonplace and well-known to your audience.

The sequence with which you present these components will determine the mood your opening creates. There are a variety of possible **beginning gambits**. You should be able to create 120 different openings just by using each component once. Add in the possibility of dropping an element, or repeating one for emphasis, and your options, while not literally limitless, are vast.

Speaker's checklist: seven beginning gambits

→ **The story gambit:** before – now – question – idea

→ **The emphatic gambit:** idea – before – now – question – idea

→ **The direct gambit:** idea – question – now

→ **The saviour gambit:** now – before – idea – question

→ **The tension gambit:** now – before – question – idea

→ **The Q&A gambit:** question – idea – before – now

→ **The hook gambit:** question – before – now – idea

Excitement, humour and sympathy: the story-teller's way

Mankind is a story-telling creature. When we hear the start of a story, we feel comfortable or exhilarated and we want to listen. So part of your toolkit must be an ability to create and tell stories. Stories are defined by having a narrative arc: at the beginning, the storyteller sets up a tension that, through a series of incidents, is eventually resolved.

STORY-TELLING AROUND THE CAMPFIRE

How to Speak so People Listen

Even the most unconventional stories – those that subvert just about any other conventions – respect that structure. Take for example the Hollywood movie *Memento*: a story that is told backwards, with each scene ending where the previous one began; the confusion we as an audience feel at the outset is resolved by the end.

The other massive benefit that the story structure gives you as a speaker is its natural ability to deliver a powerful emotional punch. In much of the speaking you will want to do – meetings, complicated conversations, presentations, even speeches – blatant emotion will feel alien and inappropriate. But when those emotions arise organically from the story you are telling, your audience won't question them: they will accept them readily because your story will create an experience that immerses each listener in their own version of it. Become a story-teller.

Speaker's checklist: story plots

Undiscovered weakness

The fatal flaw in a product or a person leads to their ultimate downfall – the basis of much tragedy and a surprising amount of comedy.

The price

A bargain is struck that seems too good to be true … and it later is shown to be just that, as a price must be paid.

Unrequited love

Love or admiration at a distance, which can never be fulfilled, is resolved either by surprising fulfilment or by eventual acceptance.

Doomed love

Love or admiration sets the protagonists up for their own demise, because it can never succeed.

▶

The trap

The hunter sets the trap and, despite many near misses, their prey is captured. The hunter and prey can each be good or evil respectively. This is one of the structures for a love story.

Undiscovered treasure

The good or talented hero is unappreciated, even despised by those near to them, until their talent or goodness is uncovered. This is another of the structures for successful love. The classic rags-to-riches stories conform to this form.

A loss

Losing something is always more poignant than never having had it.

The search for what is lost

Many quest stories are a search for what is lost – often accompanied by paying a price if it is found.

Triumph against adversity

Whether it is a monster to slay or quest to fulfil, the hero must go on a journey and face their greatest fears.

The return home

There is the potential for as much tension in the return journey and what awaits us at home as there is in the outward journey.

The solution

A puzzle or challenge is set, which the hero must solve – usually also at a personal cost.

Together in adversity

Dissimilar personalities are thrown together by a situation and must get along through a series of challenges.

The underdog

Unlikely hero turns out to be a hero nonetheless. This is a version of 'undiscovered treasure', where the hero's heroism is the treasure.

Succumbing to fear

The hero's fears lead them to an ill-advised action. This is a version of 'the price' that allows this list to have 14, not 13 items in it. The price here is intellectual honesty!

Persuasive: the three secrets of a persuasive argument

Among the many accomplishments of the great Greek thinker Aristotle was an analysis of how we persuade one another. For him, reason and logic were supreme and he argued that the soundest arguments were built from them. But he also recognised that they are rarely enough to persuade us, so he identified a trio of strategies. He said that, to make your argument persuasive, you must appeal to three domains. With any one of them missing, your appeal is weak and you may fail to persuade. His three strategies are still most commonly given their Greek names: **ethos, logos** and **pathos**.

→ **Ethos – gut:** How do we know that we can trust the speaker? It is their ethos that tells us this, and the great orators argued that we should establish this right at the start of our speaking. It answers the question: 'Why should I listen to you?' Ethos appeals to instinct – to our gut.

→ **Logos – head:** The heart of your persuasive speech needs to establish a reasoned argument that puts your evidence in a logical way. We know that this alone may not be enough to persuade, but without logos, your persuasion becomes manipulation. Logos appeals to reason – to our head.

→ **Pathos – heart:** 'Pathetic' is used today as a derogatory term, but pathos simply means an appeal to our feelings and values. This is what gives your argument its real emotional power and moves us to want to act. Use words and stories to conjure emotion. Pathos appeals to our heart.

When you build an argument carefully, using all three approaches, you will be effective. It is still possible that not everyone will be persuaded – and nor would we want to use a technique that could persuade anyone of anything – but many will. The people you persuade are those you convince of your authority to speak on the subject, who are convinced by the evidence you present and how you interpret it for them, and who are moved by your appeal to their values, their sympathy and their passions.

Ethos and the importance of character

You have either built a character that people trust or you haven't; but what matters when you are speaking – and want me to listen – is how you demonstrate your character. This gives you the credibility to speak to me. Credibility literally means the ability to be believed. How can you demonstrate that? The checklist below shows you.

Speaker's checklist: Mike's seven Cs of ethos

In trying to demonstrate your character and, hence, your credibility, there are seven Cs to apply.

Courtesy

Speaking courteously means fitting in with the social conventions that your listeners expect of you. Be respectful of your audience, be polite and observe the unwritten rules of the situation.

Clarity

To show your intellectual credibility, you must appear knowledgeable and thoughtful. Do this by using clear and direct language: words and sentences that your listener can readily understand. If you try to confuse your audience, or impress them with long words, it will backfire on you.

Candour

You need to appear trustworthy, so offer information openly and avoid bragging. Instead, own up to your weaknesses to demonstrate your strengths. Queen Elizabeth I did just this at Tilbury, before the threatened invasion by the Spanish Armada, when she said: "I know I have the body of a weak and feeble woman; but I have the heart and stomach of a king.'

Consistency

Steadiness and consistency are often taken as an important mark of character. What is most important is integrity: that you do as you say and you say as you do. This is reflected in the fairness with which you treat a situation and anyone else you are speaking about.

Congruence

You will be best able to persuade an audience when you are able to reflect their experiences and concerns. Adopting a persona that matches your audience is a powerful persuasion technique and one we see politicians strive to do continually.

Control

Credibility comes also from your ability to show restraint in acting from self-interest and, instead, focusing on the interests of your audience. Selflessness is a highly regarded character trait that demonstrates goodwill and honest intent.

Confidence

Do you have the confidence to speak directly and use strong words, rather than dilute your case with 'maybe', 'perhaps' or 'sometimes'? These words weaken your impact and fail to inspire confidence that you are sure of what you are speaking about. You also need to inspire confidence that you have the practical sense to move beyond your powerful speech and compelling arguments to advocate and do the right thing. The Greeks called this 'practical wisdom'.

Logos and the importance of reason

One of the most persuasive words in the English language is 'because'. There is a good reason for this: it signals the answer to the most powerful question that we ever ask: **'Why?'**

What question is it that toddlers and young children are continually asking – of their parents and carers, their teachers, and their friend and family? 'Why?' As we grow up, we mature, but that same question still dominates our minds. Social pressures mean that we will often suppress it, but the question is there.

And it is there in the minds of your listeners whenever you speak. So, if you don't answer it, they will worry about it. And if they are worrying about it, then they are not fully listening to you. If you want to speak so people listen, you have to answer their 'why' questions. 'Why?' asks fundamental questions about meaning and purpose. For example, in education and training, one of the most influential models for instructional design is Bernice McCarthy's 4MAT system. This advocates that the trainer or teacher starts their programme with answering this question, to fully engage their learners.

Logos requires not that you, the speaker, are credible, but that your evidence is. In creating your arguments, combine a focus on evidence from experience – facts, data – and observations with pure reasoning and logical deduction. Find strong evidence and reason from it rigorously. Present your case in a logical sequence that your audience will easily follow. Connect the dots and draw them, step by step, to an inevitable conclusion.

You can strengthen your appeal to logos by selecting compelling examples and illustrating them well, with demonstrations, diagrams, illustrations, statistics, charts, graphs, tables, props and anecdotes. Not all of these will have the same level of rigour – statistics can mislead and anecdotes can be selective – but they all form part of logos. Make sure you use them well: a confusing graph or a crowded data table can undermine your case just as much as a wrong graph or faulty data, if it leads your listeners to question your ethos.

Speaker's toolkit: applying ethos, logos and pathos to a sales pitch

Whether you are a sales person or not, you will need to 'sell' your ideas. We can learn a lot from how professionals apply the principles of ethos, logos and pathos.

Before your pitch, it's time to plan and prepare. At this stage, you will inevitably (and correctly) focus on logos: assembling the evidence and structuring the arguments that will demonstrate the superiority of your products or services. You will consider what props, graphs and pictures will support your sales process and rehearse your arguments.

Please don't forget ethos and pathos. You are going to need to form a connection with your potential customer, and establish your credibility with them. How will you do that? And when you have made your case, why will your customer buy? Probably not because of what you have said or shown them: more likely because of how they feel about what you have said or shown them. Will they feel safe, confident, excited, relieved? When you consider the 'buy emotion', you are thinking about pathos.

Your sales pitch has six steps:

Step 1 Rapport building: Ethos needs to dominate the opening of your pitch, where you build a rapport with your potential customer, demonstrating that you like and understand them, and that they can like and trust you.

Step 2 Opening statement: Emphasise your ethos by setting out, briefly, your credentials and link this to your understanding of their needs, problems or desires. This places you as a confident supporter who is on their side.

Step 3 Diagnosis: Now logos can come to the fore, with a rigorous analysis of their situation and what it will take to satisfy their needs. Show, logically, how unmet needs can have unfortunate consequences. Consequences evoke fear; a powerful reason to buy that derives directly from pathos.

Step 4 Solutions: You have evoked a need; now show that you can satisfy it. Steps 3 and 4, at the heart of your pitch, represent the 'pain and pill' approach.

Step 5 Handle objections: If you can anticipate objections, do so now: 'You are probably wondering … Well, let me answer that for you.' And then invite more objections … and more. Keep inviting objections and dealing with them until none remain. If you leave any, then once you leave the room, they will grow – and you will not have the chance to address them.

▶

Step 6 Close: Show how your product or service meets the customer's needs. Then introduce pathos into your close by conjuring how they will feel when they get the results you are able to promise or the regrets they may feel if they don't get what they need. And, because this is a sales process, when you have done that, your call to action is simple: ask for an order.

One difference between a sales pitch and many conversations or presentations is the need to follow up. Don't lose the value of your work by turning your attention to the next sale and forgetting this one.

If this process sounded familiar, take a look back to the classical oratory structure on page 61. The steps are just the same, they just have different labels.

Pathos and the importance of emotion

Story-telling is powerful because it accesses our emotional world. When you make us feel a part of the story, we empathise with the characters. Our feelings reinforce our sense of reality and our ability to recall factual elements of the narrative. Video and stunning images can do the same.

Two ways to use pathos are to:

→ evoke either positive emotions about you, your position or the course you are advocating;

→ evoke negative emotions about the alternatives.

The latter clearly carries far more risk to your ethos, but can be very powerful. Politicians tread this fine line constantly and we all recognise that they frequently trip.

From the laboratory: your choice of emotions

When working with pathos, it is as well to be aware what a wide range of emotions you have available to you. We mostly focus on 'the big ones': joy, sadness, anger, fear, grief, love and guilt, but there are lots more.

Robert Plutchik classified emotions according to their polarity (opposites), similarity and intensity.* He also noted that similar emotions combine to give further, more complex emotions and that there are four main positive emotions and four negative. The least intense forms of each emotion are far harder to distinguish (and have less rhetorical power) than their more intense siblings.

Positive emotions

→ Ecstasy, joy, serenity (opposite of sadness)

→ Vigilance, anticipation, interest (opposite of surprise)

→ Adoration, trust, acceptance (opposite of disgust)

→ Amazement, surprise, distraction (opposite of anticipation)

Negative emotions

→ Rage, anger, annoyance (opposite of fear)

→ Loathing, disgust, boredom (opposite of trust)

→ Terror, fear, apprehension (opposite of anger)

→ Grief, sadness, pensiveness (opposite of joy)

THE PLUTCHIK MODEL OF EMOTION

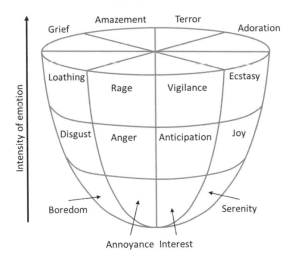

*Robert Plutchik,'A Psychoevolutionary Theory of Emotions', *Social Science Information*, 21, 1984.

The combinations

→ Joy and trust: love

→ Trust and fear: submission

→ Fear and surprise: awe

→ Surprise and sadness: disapproval

→ Sadness and disgust: remorse

→ Disgust and anger: contempt

→ Anger and anticipation: aggression

→ Anticipation and joy: optimism

The powerful impact of words

Words are the principal tools of speech. They conjure emotion, demonstrate character and build reasons. Words have power to move us, influence us and compel us. So it is important to learn how to use them well.

Plain language

There are a lot of proprietary formulae for calculating how clear your language is, taking account of how long your words are, how long your sentences are and how familiar your words are. Language is easier to listen to when you use simple words in short sentences. Simple words are real nouns and verbs, rather abstract concepts. They are short and familiar, rather than extended and intermittently occurring (sorry, long and uncommon).

But for all the sophisticated statistical tools, I favour the **five-year-old test**. Could a five-year-old understand you? If they could, then your language is at its simplest and easiest to listen to. If not, then you may want to do some work, explaining your ideas more clearly.

Good jargon: bad jargon

Not all jargon is bad, but when using jargon prevents some listeners from understanding you or, worse, from feeling part of the group, then ditch it. There is no excuse for obscuring your message behind the frosted glass of industry jargon, in-jokes, or faddish phrases such as 'blue-sky out-of-the-box synergistic leveraging of commoditised intellectual assets' – which could be translated as simply 'working together to think of new ways to use old ideas'.

→ **Poor:** We have an expedited delivery service.

→ **Good:** Our delivery is fast and efficient.

→ **Better:** We get your order to you quickly.

Descriptive language

Use your words to draw pictures and build models that people can truly grasp. Imagery has real power. When Martin Luther King wanted to talk of racial harmony, he chose to paint a picture of a time when 'little black boys and black girls will be able to join hands with little white boys and white girls'. He went further and conjured physical sensations by speaking of 'a state sweltering with the heat of oppression', contrasting it with 'an oasis of freedom and justice'.

Years of experience listening to and speaking from the pulpit made him a master at this. But you, too, can apply the principle that words do more than convey ideas; they illustrate them, sculpt them and waft them into our consciousness.

The sounds of words also help with their descriptive power: 'little' does sound like it is a little word, yet 'big' doesn't sound that big. 'Enormous' does, however, thanks to its long 'or' sound in the middle. Notice how the sound of some words will vary between accents. In southern British English, 'vast' has a long 'ahh' sound, making it sound vast indeed, while in some northern dialects, the sound is clipped down to a short 'a' (as in 'cat'), leaving the listener with anything but a vast sound. If you are preparing what to say in advance, then think about this. In general, start to notice how words sound.

For a masterclass in how words sound, read extracts from Dylan Thomas's *Under Milk Wood*. How vividly can you imagine a 'sloeblack, slow, black, crowblack, fishingboat-bobbing sea'?

Emotional language

Emotional language sounds easy – just throw in a few words for emotions and even a few descriptions of emotional behaviour. But you can be more subtle – and so more powerful – than that:

→ Your choices of pronoun confer ownership – 'We deliver our products quickly', 'You will get your goods quickly'.

→ Your use of prepositions imply relationships and distances – 'I recommend we promote Sylvia', 'Let's move Sylvia up'.

→ Using adverbs and adjectives gives priority, emphasis and nuance to your verbs and nouns – 'I need your help with this project', 'I need your insight to help with this innovative project'.

Precise language

Word power is not just about knowing lots of words. Learning exotic, esoteric, obsolescent words from a dictionary may be fun for some but it is no use if the people around you don't understand them. Instead, listen to good speakers and read good books or magazines, and notice the words that those speakers and writers use. If they use them well then you will learn how you too can use them. If they are unfamiliar, look them up, and understand how you could reuse them properly.

Powerful language

We saw earlier in this chapter how the word 'because' carries power because it answers the important question, 'Why?' There are other words that also seem to have a disproportionate power.

Speaker's checklist: power words

→ **You**, **your** – pronouns that focus your speech on your listener, just as I do in this book.

→ **Please**, **thank you**, **you're welcome** – courtesy words that say something about your character.

→ **Guarantee, safe, protect** – conjure the emotion of fear and say you can help.

→ **Proven, tested, health** – remind us that you care.

→ **Imagine, discover, learn** – evoke the emotion of curiosity.

→ **Vital, essential, key** – suggest a priority.

→ **Now, today, immediately** – do the same, in time terms.

→ **Free, discount, save** – pander to our desire to get something for nothing.

→ **Improved, better, best** – suggest merit.

→ **Control, authority, command** – focus on our need to either be in charge, or know who is.

Puny language

Some words display a lack of confidence and thus undermine your authority. Why should I listen to you if you are not sure? 'Maybe', 'possibly', 'probably', 'might', 'perhaps' and 'could' all weaken your language, and 'sort of', 'you know', 'it seems', 'I think' and 'I suppose' are wasted words at best: at worst they betray doubt. Often, we say 'I hope' because 'I don't know'.

Deceptive language

It gets worse, because some words can mean precisely the opposite:

→ **'I'm sure'** often means 'I'm not sure', as does 'I think'.

→ **'Honestly'** sometimes means 'I'm holding something back'.

→ **'Don't worry'** means 'You should, because I will'.

→ **'As you know'** can mean 'I think I forgot to tell you'.

Dangerous language

Some words hold particular dangers for a speaker. The word 'but' is small, but can easily trip you up. As soon as we hear it, our mind starts to discount what we have just heard and prepares ourselves for the truth. 'You're a great person, but ...' Try replacing it with 'and' when you want both halves of your sentence to count: 'You're a great person and I would love it if you could …'

The word 'promise' – as politicians frequently find – can get you into all sorts of trouble. This may concern us less here, because that trouble is often long after the conversation is over. But if you want to avoid a commitment you cannot control, try 'I am going to work hard to achieve …' instead of 'I promise …'

No language

At some times, the greatest asset for a speaker is no words at all: silence. Slowing down, pausing and stopping …

When you pause, your listener wonders: what next? This creates tension, mystery and suspense. Slowing down and pausing gives your words weight. They become more deliberate; less casual. They build ethos.

From the laboratory: Albert Mehrabian and the persistence of nonsense

Albert Mehrabian conducted two of the best known and most widely misunderstood and misrepresented experiments.*

In his first experiment, working with Morton Wiener, speakers listened to words conveying liking, neutrality or dislike, spoken in different tonalities. Subjects were asked to rate the attitude of the speaker. They found that subjects used the tone far more than the content when deciding how positive the speaker was.

The second experiment, done with Susan Ferris, asked subjects to interpret the emotion in a recording of a speaker voicing a neutral word with different intonations, conveying liking, neutrality or dislike. At the same time subjects were shown photos of actors portraying one of the same three emotions. Subjects rated the emotion of the speech-photo pair. When there was a mismatch, subjects chose the emotion in the photo more often than the voice.

*Albert Mehrabian, *Silent Messages: Implicit communication of emotions and attitudes*, 2nd edition (Wadsworth, 1981).

How to Speak so People Listen

In combining the results of these two studies, Mehrabian and his collaborators concluded that, when the message conveyed emotional content and there was a mismatch between what the speaker says and how they say it:

→ 7 per cent of the interpretation derives from the words;

→ 38 per cent from the vocal patterns;

→ 55 per cent from the facial expression.

Note that this is not the same as asserting that words convey only 7 per cent of a message. If this were true, what hope for Charles Dickens or Jane Austen? It does mean that when we are uncertain, it is our face and our intonation that give us away. And when we seek to influence, a flat delivery has far less impact than an animated, committed, impassioned presentation.

Mehrabian himself has been at pains to repudiate the simplistic interpretation that many books and trainers give. His work only applies when all three channels are visible and there is a mild mismatch between the impressions we get from them. Indeed, he found that if the incongruence between the words and the expression is too great, we suspect that the expression is being faked.

Does Mehrabian's work tell us that words hardly matter? Not at all. It tells us that ethos and pathos matter as much as logos, and that words are not the only way we assess them.

Watch a great video on this by Creativity Works, at **http://bit.ly/ BustingMehrabianMyth**

The YES/NO of getting your message across

YES

→ Make your speaking compelling, persuasive and powerful.

→ Use a clear structure and logical sequence of ideas to compel your audience to keep listening.

→ Remember that classical oratory can teach you a lot.

→ Use all three strategies of ethos (character), logos (reason) and pathos (emotion) to appeal to your listeners' guts, heads and hearts.

→ Use plain, descriptive and powerful language.

NO

→ Avoid an argument becoming a fight – focus on agreement, rather than being right.

→ Remember that mismatching your audience's expectations will be a breach of decorum and damage your ethos.

→ Avoid puny words, dangerous language and jargon that excludes listeners from understanding you fully.

Get results

Chapter Six

Sometimes you need to speak at levels 5 and 6: so that people remember, and they think or do what you want them to. If you want people to remember and act on your ideas, your speaking must have the power to secure an emotional commitment and etch itself on the memory. This chapter examines the psychology of how to portray your confidence, win that commitment by honing your powers of persuasion, and use some basic techniques to make your message memorable.

Compelling	Level 1. How to speak so people listen
	Level 2. How to speak so people understand
Persuasive	Level 3. How to speak so people understand, as you intend them to
	Level 4. How to speak so people agree with you
Powerful	Level 5. How to speak so people remember what you want them to
	Level 6. How to speak so people think or do what you want them to

Influence and beyond

In preceding chapters, you have already read a lot about the basics of persuasion. You need to:

→ Start by making a strong and positive first impression.

→ Build rapport and gain trust (we'll look at this in detail in Chapter 7).

→ Take an interest in what the other person has to say, asking good questions.

→ Demonstrate your interest with good listening (we'll examine listening in Chapter 7).

→ Have an interesting and carefully considered message to convey.

→ Articulate your message in a structured way to make it compelling to listen to …

→ … and do so clearly, so that your listener understands what you are saying, as you mean them to.

Now, we just want to add to the power of your influence with additional techniques that penetrate the deepest levels of your listener's understanding to change the way they think.

The levels of understanding

Let's take a look at a simple model of how people understand their world, and therefore your message. It represents different layers of interpretation, from the most superficial to the deepest. Please notice that increasing depth has no implications for increasing accuracy. Our understanding can be even less 'correct' at the deeper level, but it will be harder to reshape.

LEVELS OF UNDERSTANDING

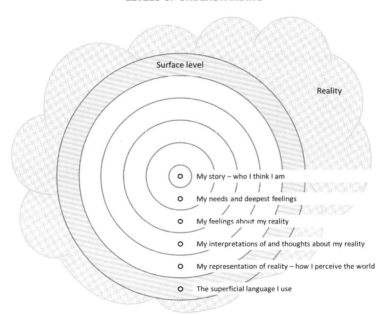

Surface level

Reality

○ My story – who I think I am

○ My needs and deepest feelings

○ My feelings about my reality

○ My interpretations of and thoughts about my reality

○ My representation of reality – how I perceive the world

○ The superficial language I use

To influence me, you must affect my understanding at one or more of the levels below the outermost, surface level. The deeper you can penetrate, the more profoundly you will influence me. Let's review the six levels and what they mean.

Superficial level: the superficial language I use

We use language to express our understanding of the world – sometimes with care and precision, other times not. Unknown to ourselves, we sometimes use language to obscure what we are really thinking and feeling. To this we add social and emotional signals that further complicate understanding of what we say. The problem is that not only does this surface level of communication obscure what I say to you, it influences how I think about things: maybe fooling or misleading myself. This surface level will be very important to us in Chapter 7, when we consider the implications of speaking that comes entirely from here. We will call this **outer-circle speaking**.

Representational level: my representation of reality

The next level of understanding is how I represent reality to myself: how I interpret the evidence of my senses. This is not the real world as it is, but as I filter it through the mental filters we discussed in Chapter 2. I deform the information I gather, and so possibly misunderstand some of it. I select what information to pay attention to and retain, thus creating a limited understanding from a specific perspective. And I draw generalisations from what I hear and see – some of which may be false.

Interpretational level: my thoughts about and interpretations of my reality

I base my thoughts and interpretations on my representation of reality, so any errors are carried deeper. But now, my experiences, beliefs, values and prejudices further deform, select and generalise my representations – compounding any error.

Emotional level: my feelings about my reality

I react to my interpretations emotionally too, affecting my mood and my openness to what you have to say. If you can affect my feelings intentionally, then you can influence me profoundly.

How to Speak so People Listen

Motivational level: my needs and deepest feelings

My present emotions are also influenced by my needs and my deepest feelings. If you could affect those, you can make permanent changes to the way I react. When your speaking addresses my beliefs and my values, you can not only change the way I perceive the world, but motivate me to change what I will do.

Personal level: my story

At my core is my story: who I think I am and what I think I am supposed to do in the world. It is a narrative that answers all my deepest inner questions, such as 'Who?' and 'Why?' It therefore fundamentally drives my values and beliefs. If your speaking can influence my story, you can change me.

How the levels influence one another

All these levels are interconnected; influencing one another. The primary influence runs from the inside outwards: your story influences your needs, which influence your feelings, which influence how you interpret your reality, which affects the filters that influence how you represent reality, which influences the language you use to communicate. But there is also feedback in the other direction. You hear the words you use and they influence how you represent reality, which influences how you think about it, which influences your feelings, which influence your needs, which influence your story about who you are.

Speaker's toolkit: using the levels of understanding to understand communication

The first image overleaf represents the way that our communication is based on our interpretation of only one part of reality.

When I communicate with you, we must have something in common – our parts of reality must overlap, and I can only understand you to the extent that you can create awareness of your part of reality, so that it becomes part of my reality too. Our ability to fully understand one another relies upon the extent to which we ▶

are able to overlap our levels of understanding. Our communication is constrained by differing interpretations of different parts of reality. This is illustrated in the second image.

MY COMMUNICATION OF MY REALITY

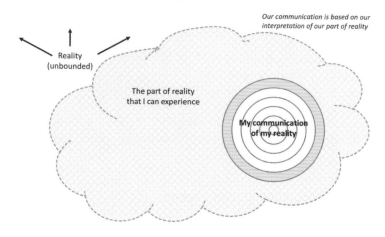

DRAWING TOGETHER OUR LEVELS OF UNDERSTANDING

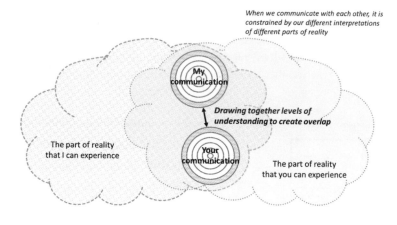

The power to get results

The power to get results arises from the six levels of understanding. It can be seen as a power formula:

Speaking power =
interest + insight + influence + impact + impulsion + inspiration

Interest

Nothing really trumps the power of self-interest to drive behaviour, but to get through the superficial level of understanding you must first pique my interest.

Insight

Next, you can use the power of insight to help me reconfigure the way I represent reality.

Influence

To alter how I interpret the world, deploy the power of influence.

Impact

We have already seen that the emotions that stories and language can carry can have a profound impact on your emotional level.

Impulsion

At the motivational level, power comes from your ability to tap into my beliefs and values to impel me to make changes.

Inspiration

If you can deploy the power of inspiration successfully, you can inspire me to change who I am.

The tools to get results

Changing other people's understanding at the deeper levels – influencing and beyond – requires some advanced skills in your communication. To help you, we will tease out some of the techniques available, using four headings:

1 Respect

2 Psychology

3 Persuasion

4 Memory

Respect

I have tried to stress the need to be respectful throughout this book, but I want to emphasise the point. The deeper you seek to go in affecting someone's thoughts and feelings, the more challenging it can be. If you do not do so respectfully, you will quickly encounter resistance. Think of respect as a lubricant for complicated conversations that are uncomfortable for both parties.

When you show me respect, you help build my self-esteem. This gives me the confidence to move away from the solid ground of my own certainty. The less self-esteem I have, the more tightly I cling to what I believe are the certainties in my life. One of the most profound sources of resistance to new realities and new thinking is fear.

You build respect when you are able to learn how people perceive their world and honour their perceptions. You may not have formed the same story about the world as they have (as I described in Chapter 2), but you must understand and respect that story. You do this, of course, by asking questions. Questions encourage dialogue and invite, in a less threatening manner, the other person to examine their own story and evaluate it. Challenging their story, on the other hand, will cause an immediate reaction.

How you ask your questions, comment on the answers and share your perceptions, will have a big effect on how much I feel you respect me. If you can do so in a way that matches my natural styles of speech, I will feel comfortable and respected; if you don't, I will feel a clash. This goes beyond the superficialities of speech, such as how quickly we speak and the sort of words we choose, right down to the way that language reflects our **thought patterns**.

Thought patterns

For a short while, I am going to use the phrase 'thought patterns' in a very specific way: to denote particular ways of thinking about the world. We each have a number of different thought patterns, like a pattern of different 'chunk sizes'. Some of us will assess a situation as a whole: considering, evaluating and describing to others the big picture – the whole canvas. Other people, in the same situation, will zoom in on the little details, noticing what is where and how they relate to one another.

So, for example, Alfie and Betty arrive together at the same large event, hosted in the ballroom of a hotel. When Chris talks to each of them afterwards, they each give a very different account of the same experience.

Alfie: 'We went into a large bustling room filled with the noise of dozens of conversations. There was a lot going on, with people eating, drinking and chatting, so I decided to wander around and get a feel for the layout of the room.'

Betty: 'We had to push past a group of people in smart suits, talking earnestly about something, and everywhere I looked there were other groups, who already had drinks and food. I set off for the back of the room, where there were some people on their own at the buffet.'

Can you appreciate the different thought patterns that represented the same event in distinct ways? If you can hear these subtleties and reflect them in your conversation and questioning, you are not only respecting the other person's way of reading the world, but they will understand you more easily.

To Alfie, ask: 'How interesting did you find the event? What sort of people attended? What was the food like?' Question him about broad themes.

To Betty, ask: 'What interesting conversations did you have? Who was there? What food did they serve?' Encourage her to pick out details.

Speaker's toolkit: tuning in to thought patterns

There are lots of different thought patterns you can tune into. Let's list a few that are easier to notice.

Chunks

Do people notice and talk about big chunks – a view from the gallery – or small details – a ringside seat? Some people start at one extreme and shift perspective as they speak, either zooming in from global to specific, or panning out from detail to panorama.

Similarity

Our brains notice discrepancies, but we don't all focus on them: some do and will talk about 'what is different about …' while others prefer to focus on 'what is similar about …'

Direction

When we speak about what is important to us, some will be more preoccupied with what draws them towards what they want while others tend to be focused on moving away from what they want to avoid.

Position

Some people prefer to talk about events as if they are a remote observer, separated from what is happening. Others tend to describe the events as if they are a part of them and are associated with what happens.

Senses

When we want to take in information, evaluate a situation or convince ourselves of something, we need to use our senses. But which do we prefer? We each use all of them, but in different balance, with our own preferences for seeing, hearing, reading, doing – or even sniffing out – a problem. We give these preferences away in the language we use.

Interests

What interests you about something? It will probably be a mixture of things, but some will rate more highly than others. Pick your favourite hobby or pastime: what do you like about it? The activity, the things, the people, the information or the places where you do it? Which ones you talk about will tell me which ones to comment on.

Meaning

Some people speak absolutely literally – they say what they mean and mean what they say: 'I am thirsty.' Others are less literal: they prefer you to draw inferences from what they say: 'I wonder if there is a bar at this event.'

Psychology

Have you ever noticed when you go to a restaurant that the waiter or waitress rarely takes an order for dessert when you order starters and a main course? Why is that? Maybe it is because when you look at the cost of the whole meal, a dessert seems extravagant – especially as you have already ordered a lot of food. After your main course, things seem different: you've enjoyed yourself and you want to stay. And you've now spent a lot of money, so what difference will a little extra make? Maybe restaurants use psychology to encourage us to spend more.

Put a small cost next to a big cost and it looks even smaller: insignificant. Car salesmen know that, and so do shop assistants who sell you a scarf with your new dress or a tie with your new suit. This is the **black and white effect**: we don't evaluate things on their own, we place them in the context of other things. If we were to consider them entirely on their merits we may make a different decision.

Psychologists love collecting all these **hidden persuaders**: the psychological techniques that can help us make choices without us being consciously aware of their influence. Sadly, it is outside of the scope of this book to examine this fascinating topic in depth; happily, however, my book *Brilliant Influence* covers it thoroughly.

From the laboratory: six experimentally tested psychological methods to influence and persuade

I'm gorgeous, fly me

The more I like you, the more I will trust you. So make yourself likeable or, if you can't make yourself likeable enough, attach yourself, your products or your argument to someone I do like. This is why advertisers use celebrities.

Eight out of ten cat owners

We all want to conform, and experiments show that we will even step outside our normal behavioural norms in order to fit in with a social group. We do what the people around us do, so show me others who do or think as you want me to.

Your doctor would tell you to

A credible source is a trustworthy source, so support your argument with badges of authority, such as your experience and testimonials, the name and title of a prominent researcher, or symbols like a smart suit for executives or a stethoscope for doctors.

The sale must end on Friday

As soon as something becomes rare, we crave it. It isn't just for its beauty that gold is valued, but also for its rarity. Far less useful than iron, it is also far more scarce. When we fear to lose what we have, we act to protect it – especially when what we have is an opportunity.

I've scratched your back, now you scratch mine

Our sense of fairness and equity drives us to want to reciprocate a favour, so if you do something for me or make a concession in your demands, I will feel an inner pressure to reciprocate. That's why a salesperson will make a big deal of how hard they had to work to get their manager to agree to that extra discount: you owe them one – the least you can do is say 'yes' and buy it.

Shock, awe and laughter

Anything that suddenly interrupts your normal thinking pattern will lower your defences to persuasion. 'How much is it?' you ask. 'It's very good value – only 650 pennies' the shop-keeper says. The unexpectedness of this answer made a big difference to buying choices in one experiment. More people bought because they didn't fully evaluate a price that was actually high!

Persuasion

We saw in the last chapter how the Greeks discovered the three secrets of a persuasive argument: ethos, or character; logos, or reason; and pathos, or emotion. Let's go one step further and investigate how to structure an explicitly persuasive argument or proposal.

The structure

Let us start with a very simple and instructive technique that was a favourite among Greek orators. They would start by stating something we all know and cannot therefore dispute: 'We should not trust liars.' This is the **commonplace**. Then they would state a conclusion that they draw from the commonplace: 'Therefore we cannot trust the government.' This is the **inference**.

In doing this, we break the rules of formal logic, by missing out a step that rigorous reasoning requires: 'The government has lied.' Logically, therefore, the inference is suspect, but the rhetorical impact remains, due to the power of the implied 'because', which we saw in Chapter 5.

Step 1: Commonplace

All persuasion starts from some common ground: a knowledge or belief that both parties share. Your first job is to establish what this commonplace is.

Step 2: Your case

Now make your case. Keep it simple, focusing on one or two strong points in favour. If you make too many points, the impact of each is diluted and the total effect is less, not more, impact. Focus your evidence on what is most relevant for your listener.

Step 3: The argument

Accept that the other person has a different point of view and acknowledge it, to create a tension between the evidence you have put and their understanding, beliefs or interpretation.

Step 4: Resolution

The wrong thing to do is to refute the other person's case. This would turn an argument into a conflict. Instead, offer a resolution that reconciles your evidence with their position.

When we feel the kind of inner argument you have created, that creates what psychologists call **cognitive dissonance**. This is the brain-ache we feel when we try to hold to conflicting views. We are compelled to resolve it. One way is to think 'I was wrong'. This does not happen easily. The easier alternative is 'Your evidence is wrong'. Since you believe it is right, we have a conflict. If you can you can show me how to reconcile the two, I can get rid of my brain-ache to both of our satisfaction.

Speaker's tip: the 'one more thing' technique

When you say something like 'Oh, there's one more thing; something I may not have told you' or 'There's something you may not have been aware of', you are giving me a marvellous way out of my brain-ache. Now I don't have to change my mind: I was right all along … given what I knew. 'Oh,' I can say, 'if I'd known that …'

The persuasive elements

What makes a case persuasive? The answer depends on who you are and what matters to you. Earlier, we saw how you can be respectful by tuning into my thought patterns. It will also help you to be more persuasive. Other persuasive elements are:

Criteria

Some people are persuaded by value – wanting to secure something with minimal cost. Others don't count the cost as long as they get the right quality. Others focus more on convenience, some on timeliness and some don't care about these as long as they can minimise the risk of getting it wrong. You can only persuade me if you know what my criteria are.

Salespeople

Salespeople know that to persuade a potential buyer they have to convince them of three things:

1 The product or service will benefit the customer (**what's in it for me?**).
2 It will do so more than its rivals or competitors (**mine's better than theirs**).
3 It will work for them as promised (**it will do what it says on the tin**).

Marketers

Marketers and advertisers are keen to persuade us to buy too, but they are not close enough to the customer to address their concerns directly. They use the acronym **SPACED** to help them remember six common reasons why people will choose one product over another. They then identify which one or two of them will make their product stand out against its competitors.

A good example is in car adverts. You will easily be able to find examples of adverts (TV or print) that highlight each of these:

Security or **safety** – how safe are you with this?

Performance – how well does it do its job?

Appearance – how good does it look?

Convenience – how easy is it to use?

Economy – how much does it cost to buy and own?

Durability – how long will it last?

From the laboratory: persuade different people in different ways

In a study of 1,684 executives, Robert Miller and Gary Williams found a consistent pattern of five readily distinguished decision-making styles:*

→ **Followers:** who want to be sure somebody else whom they trust has tested the idea successfully first.

→ **Charismatics:** who are captivated by new ideas, yet rely on others to understand the details.

→ **Sceptics:** who really only trust their own instincts and want every assertion validated.

→ **Thinkers:** who will systematically examine each ramification of every alternative.

→ **Controllers:** who like to feel in control and will only adopt ideas they themselves have generated.

Miller and Williams found that each of these styles of decision-maker is best persuaded in a different way. To summarise a whole book here is impossible, but as a flavour to whet your appetite:

→ **Followers:** Focus on proof that your proposal will work and evidence that others have tried it successfully before. Use words such as 'expertise' and 'safe'.

→ **Charismatics:** Present ideas, then focus on straightforward facts and results. Give them time to think, and use words such as 'clear' and 'action'.

*Gary Williams and Robert Miller, 'Change the Way You Persuade', *Harvard Business Review*, May 2002. The study was also the basis of their book, *The Five Paths to Persuasion*.

→ **Sceptics:** Use arguments grounded in practical reality and focus on credibility. Allow them to challenge, and then respond calmly. Use word such as 'grasp' and 'trust'.

→ **Thinkers:** Respect their intelligence, focusing on data and robustness of analysis. Show your methodology and be open about gaps and weaknesses. Use words such as 'proof' and 'plan'.

→ **Controllers:** Give a structured argument but avoid pressing the case: let them adopt it or not. Then feed them supporting evidence. Use words such as 'reason' and 'power'.

Memory

You can only get long-term results from your speaking if people remember what you say. And they won't always have a notebook or tablet device to hand to record it, so you need to be able to lock your message into their memory.

First, when you want people to remember something particular, alert your audience. You can do this by saying something like 'You may want to make a note of this'. That is also a tactic to use when you are asking someone to commit to doing something.

One of the commonest reasons people let us down is that they simply forget. And they do that because, when they say yes, they barely notice it. On the other hand, if you can wake up Jiminy Cricket, their conscience, by saying 'Thank you for saying you'll do this', then not only will they remember better, but the **Jiminy Cricket effect** will work for you to keep them honest.

The same cognitive dissonance that we saw earlier will also help enforce promises people make to you. If you alert my conscience to the fact that I am making a commitment to you then, as long as I see myself as being an honest person of true integrity (and most people do), Jiminy Cricket will nag at me if he senses that I am about to renege on my promise.

The speaker's filing cabinet that you read about in Chapter 4 is a good way to prime your listeners to remember what you are going to say. After that, it is down to you to make your content memorable. Luckily, you have five shots at doing that.

Speaker's checklist: five ways to make what you say memorable

Our brains are primed to remember some things – whether ideas or events. These are the first, the last, the recurring, the novel and the ones we engage with.

If there is one single message you must get across and have your audience retain, use as many of these techniques as possible.

Primacy

Include the message in your opening words, as early as possible.

Recency

We remember the last thing we hear too, so include it at the end of your summing up.

Frequency

What we hear more often, we remember, so repeat your message throughout.

These first three techniques are, of course, the basis of the old advice: 'Tell 'em what you are going to tell 'em; then tell 'em it; then tell 'em what you told 'em.' However, there's more …

Novelty

Anything that takes us by surprise, or is unusual, is more likely to stick in the memory. So, 'Tell 'em in a shocking, creative or outrageous way'. Use demonstrations, humour, video or anecdote to emphasise your message.

Activity

Finally, we are also far more likely to remember something we have been actively involved in. This is because it activates a far wider range of neural pathways. 'Don't just tell 'em: engage 'em.'

How to Speak so People Listen

The YES/NO of getting results

YES

→ Remember that people understand their world and your words at different levels.

→ Show your listener respect.

→ Use the power formula: *Speaking power = interest + insight + influence + impact + impulsion + inspiration.*

→ Deploy psychology to influence and persuade.

→ Understand the six persuaders in SPACED.

→ Notice and try to emulate other people's thought patterns.

NO

→ Don't for one moment think that your representation of reality is 'right'.

→ Don't assume that, because you said something, you have been understood.

→ Don't rely on one approach for every person you want to persuade.

The four situations

Part Three

Focus on conversations

Chapter Seven

Conversations are the most intimate use of speech. We are engaged in them continually from our earliest days to our final hours. You use them for idle chatter or with a clear purpose. You converse in person and on the phone. Your conversations are easy or complicated, conveying everything from shopping lists to love, and from good news to breakdowns.

Because of their familiarity, we think we understand them. So why is it that, so often, people don't hear what you say – or they hear it in a way that really surprises you? Let's find out.

The art of conversation

Conversations are intimate. So, to make them as effective as possible, focus on the 'you' in communication. When you put the word 'you' into your conversation, you alert the other person that they need to listen, you prepare them to take responsibility for how they respond, and you make them feel at the heart of your concerns.

The **you principle** goes further. When holding a conversation, people's favourite topic is usually themselves. So when you can focus the conversation around my interests and around me, I am likely to consider you a good conversationalist. Take an interest in me, listen carefully and refrain from judging me.

Start a new conversation on safe ground by asking about something safe, such as impressions or facts. Feelings and emotions, on the other hand, may be too intimate a subject, and might scare me off. When you go somewhere where you are likely to need to start conversations, especially with people you don't know, it pays to have a stock of conversation starters and some familiarity with current events.

Speaker's checklist: conversation starters

Most conversation starters are on a spectrum from situational to personal. Since the 'you principle' tells us that you should focus on the other person, rather than on yourself, that means me.

- → Make an observation about where we are: "There is a good turn-out today, for a mid-week event.'

- → Ask me something about where we are or some specific feature of it: "Do you know anything about the history of this building? It's so impressive.'

- → Ask me about how I came here: "This place is nice and central; how did you come here tonight?'

- → Ask me what drew me to come here:' 'What appealed to you most about this event?'

- → Express an interest in speaking with me:' 'I couldn't help noticing you and wondered if you would mind if I introduce myself?'

- → Make an observation about me (avoiding anything that might embarrass me): "I am interested in what you said earlier on. Your comments were thought-provoking.'

- → Ask me something about what I am wearing or have with me: "I see you are carrying Mike's new book – what are your impressions of it?'

- → Ask me something you think I might know about: "When you are writing a book, do you have a process you follow?'

- → Ask me something about myself: "What interests you most about the work you do?'

When you want to ask me a question about myself, the best ones open up a whole realm of new information beyond the scope of the question itself. 'If you could travel to one place in the world, where would you most want to go to?' will open up a conversation about the place, the interests that attract me there, our past experiences of travel and my attitudes to all sorts of things from culture to food to transport.

I suggest you avoid those 'clever' questions, which make people feel they need a 'clever' answer, until you are both comfortable with one another: 'What would be the one statement that summarises your philosophy on life?' might simply elicit: 'Don't ask questions that make people feel inadequate.'

Conversational genius, Leil Lowndes, gives excellent advice, noting that 'So, what do you do?' is another question that can cause embarrassment – as well as marking you out as potentially a relentless networker or shamelessly looking for opportunities. Far better, she advises, to ask: 'How do you spend most of your time?' Her book *How to Talk to Anyone* is a conversationalist's goldmine.

Once you get started, carrying on a conversation becomes easy. If you find yourself stalling, you can either restart with another conversation starter, or, better, pick up on something I said earlier on and either comment on it, or ask me about it. There are four basic conversational skills that keep a conversation going along nicely:

1 Rapport with your conversation partner.
2 Appropriate eye-contact.
3 Serious listening.
4 Being comfortable with pauses and silence.

If your conversation is going well, it can be hard to end it. The best ways are always to express your pleasure in the conversation and politely but confidently excuse yourself. You really don't have to apologise for having other concerns in your life. 'It has been a pleasure speaking with you. Now, I need to get home/prepare for my talk/get some food/find someone ...'

If you are interrupted, on the other hand, perhaps by a phone, then you should apologise for that: 'I am really sorry: I have enjoyed speaking with you and I wish I didn't have to take this call. Unfortunately, I must.' Notice here, how I have avoided the 'but': 'I have enjoyed talking, but I must go' weakens the first part significantly.

Now let's examine the four basic conversational skills in some more depth.

Rapport

Rapport is the dance we create, carrying the parts of a conversation from you to me and back, constantly building our relationship and empathising with one another's perceptions. Rapport connects us, helps us to understand each other and creates a sense of trust. Anything that you can do to strengthen rapport can also help people to listen to you.

Rapport is based on similarity, so to strengthen rapport, you need to find and emphasise those points of similarity between you and the people who are listening, whether it is one conversation partner or an audience of hundreds. Remember:

'People like people who are like themselves.'

Very simple outward cues can help at the outset. Dressing in a way that conforms to people's expectations, for example, or an opening statement that begins: 'Like you, I …'

Agreeing with and building upon things the other person says will increase your rapport, but what do you do when you disagree? The secret is to be honest in a way that keeps rapport: 'I can grasp what you mean, so let me see how you feel about this interpretation.' Or how about: 'I'd like to understand better how you made that assessment: can you say more about the difference between …?'

Speaker's toolkit: building rapport

Your toolkit for rapport building is … you.

Body position

In conversation, the orientation of your body to mine (turn to face me for greatest impact) and its proximity can make or break rapport. If I don't look comfortable facing you directly, then allow yourself to stand slightly to one side too. Get the distance wrong and I will either feel you are too close and familiar or too distant and cold. Luckily, we all have a fairly well-tuned sense of the bubble around us – at about arm's length.

I referred a little while ago to Leil Lowndes. Of all her tips, my favourite is 'The big-baby pivot'. When someone comes towards you, don't just look at them and don't just turn your head, but swing your whole body round to greet them and give them a powerful smile that says 'Thank you for coming over to me; I am looking forward to speaking with you'.

Posture, gesture and expression

Watch two people deep in conversation at a coffee shop or bar. You will see matching postures, gestures that look the same (made almost simultaneously) and similar expressions passing over each person's face. We do this naturally when we are in rapport. When we do it deliberately, picking one or two aspects at first, we strengthen rapport.

▶

Vocal patterns

All the normal patterns of how we speak can be shared. When you match the volume, pace and tone of your speaking to mine, you will increase our rapport and make it more comfortable for me to listen to you. The one aspect to avoid is accent: since very few of us have a precise enough sense of accent, attempting to mimic it comes across as disrespectful – even mocking.

Word choice

Notice some of the words I use a lot and pepper them occasionally into your speech. This will make me feel at home with your turns of phrase. They will feel comfortingly familiar to me. A common example is the words we use to describe how we understand one another. Some people see what you are saying and understand your point of view (my own favourite), while others hear you clearly, so that your words ring true. Some get a feel for your angle on things and grasp your meaning, while others like to sniff out the essence of your argument to see if it smells sweet or if it stinks. If you can use the same senses in your speech – visual, auditory, bodily or smell – then the other person will see, hear, grasp or sniff out your message quickly.

The not-so-royal 'we'

Of all the pronouns, 'we', 'us', 'our' and 'ours' are the ones that confer intimacy. Use them to build rapport when we are talking so that we can feel like our friendship is starting to develop and we can readily agree if someone challenges us.

From the laboratory: mirror neurons, empathy and rapport

In the late 1980s and the 1990s, scientists at the University of Parma in Italy gave us a new and controversial insight into the workings of our brains. We had known for a long time that when we move, motor command neurons fire in our brain. And when we are touched, neurons fire in the somatosensory cortex of our brain. What Giacomo Rizzolatti and his colleagues discovered is that a smaller number of neurons also fire when we see someone else move, and also when we see someone else being touched.*

This means that when I see you in a particular posture, making a specific gesture, or adopting an expression, it causes motor neurons to fire in my brain. I get a sense of how it feels to be doing what you are doing: I get a sense of what it is like to be you.

While the interpretation of what these so-called 'mirror neurons' mean and how they work is still being actively researched and hotly debated by neuroscientists and psychologists, it is clear that there is a neurological basis for rapport and empathy. It is as if the barriers between us are less when we observe one another closely and when we adopt similar movements.

Eye-contact

Eye-contact is a critical part of the body language, which makes or breaks rapport between people. As a speaker, you need to be aware that some people will listen to you most comfortably when they are holding eye-contact with you; while other feel most at ease by looking away. So there is no 'right' amount of eye-contact: there is just what is right for the person you are speaking with. Use your ability to sense when other people become uncomfortable to tune the frequency and depth of your eye-contact, so they feel completely at ease. Break contact as soon as you detect any awkwardness. Go back to Chapter 4 (page 47) if you want to remind yourself how to know the right moment to break eye-contact.

Serious listening

Perhaps the deepest need we all feel is for someone to understand us and honour our emotions, by listening to us and acknowledging how

*G. di Pellegrino, L. Fadiga, L. Fogassi, V. Gallese and G. Rizzolatti, 'Understanding Motor Events: A neurophysiological study', *Experimental Brain Research*, 91, 1992.

LISTENING LEVELS

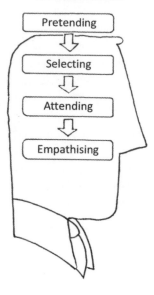

we feel. The problem is that, for something most of us do every day, listening is something a lot of us are not very good at.

We listen at four distinct levels:

Pretending

The shallowest level of listening is merely pretending. There is a superficial awareness of the speaking going on, which has only the most cursory effect on us. This is hardly listening at all; it is not respectful, and will probably be recognised for what it is by the other person.

Selecting

The human brain is able to listen in part to two conversations at once, and we frequently do: selecting which to pay more attention to and which to scan for important cues. All I pick up is some minor elements of what you are saying, so that if there is something important, I can swap attention to you. The commonest alternative voice, if it is not the conversation on the other side of the room or the TV in the corner, is the voice in my own head.

From the laboratory: dichotic listening

The **cocktail party effect** is our ability to select one conversation from many going on in the same room. Donald Broadbent and Colin Cherry studied this by feeding different information into each ear. They called it **dichotic listening**. They found that we can select which channel we wish to focus on, and can also swap channel if personally significant information appears in the neglected channel. This is akin to listening to the radio while your relative talks to you on the phone. As soon as they mention something important, you switch your attention from the radio to the telephone.

Attending

Fully attentive listening allows me to hear all your words and for them to affect my thoughts and interpretations. As I fully engage with your interpretation of reality, it may also start to affect my feelings. Active listening, where you participate fully and perhaps even make notes, is at this level.

Empathising

Now I am at the deepest level of listening of all, open to your emotions and allowing them to affect me. Consequently, my feelings and even my sense of reality may change through listening to you, and I can sense your needs and feelings as a result.

The question that arises is how can you listen at the attending and empathising levels?

How to listen

While much of listening is automatic, the following ten steps can turn it into a conscious activity that you can practice and perfect. Each step overcomes one of the barriers to good listening.

Step 1: Become curious

A sense of curiosity helps you overcome the barrier of your certainty about the world. Ask a question that truly interests you.

Step 2: Engage

Face me, make eye-contact, and remove all distractions. If you have a laptop open, close it – even when you are on the phone. This helps you to overcome the barrier of separateness and allows your mirror neurons to dissolve the emotional boundary between us.

Step 3: Put yourself out of the way

You have opinions, ideas, beliefs, values and prejudices. These create a barrier to hearing what *I* say by filtering my words through *your* reality. If you can mentally set these aside and resist the temptation to judge me, you will be better able to understand me instead.

Step 4: Silence your inner voice

Your inner voice, or **self-talk**, is a barrier to listening. While you are listening to yourself, you are not concentrating on me. Turn it off and give yourself permission to respond *when it's your turn*.

Step 5: ... and still your body

Movement is a distraction to my speaking and your listening. Remove it by becoming still, curbing your fidgeting and halting your doodling.

Step 6: Become aware of your listening

The next barrier to listening is that your brain can work faster than I can speak (four times as fast, it is often reported). So, your mind will wander unless you give it something constructive to do. Become aware of the quality of your listening, and:

→ notice key words and phrases that I use;

→ spot what I emphasise and what I avoid;

→ notice conflicts between my words, tone of voice, expression and body language;

→ pay attention to all channels of my body language: gesture, posture and voice;

→ listen between the lines … to what is not said, as well as what is.

Step 7: Let me know you are listening

Use nods, smiles, the echoing of gestures and simple phrases and sounds such as 'I see' and 'uh-huh' to keep me confident that you are still engaged.

Step 8: When I stop – think

Allow yourself time to think before you respond. We will return to silence later, but this is about the 'need to respond quickly' barrier that puts pressure on you to answer before you fully process what I have said. If I have said something important, I don't want a quick response: I want a considered, respectful response.

Step 9: Repeat, rephrase and summarise

Repeat the essence of what I said, using some of the same key words and phrases you heard at step 6. This will emphasise to me that you were listening and that you 'got it' – even if you didn't. If you need to clarify, only after repeating my own words should you test your own interpretations by rephrasing: 'When you said you feel "helpless", do you mean you don't know what to do next?' 'No,' I might reply, 'I mean that I know what to do, but I also know it may have no effect at all.' When you are sure you understand me, you may want to summarise what I have said.

Step 10: Go to the edge

If I am not confident enough to speak about what really matters, you may need to take me to the edge, to make it easier for me to take the leap. Do this by carefully speculating about what I may be feeling. Invite me to assess your interpretation – which is easier than starting from nothing.

From the laboratory: listening can really make a difference

In a 2012 study by Daniel Ames and colleagues Lily Maissen and Joel Brockner, workers rated colleagues on measures of listening skills, verbal skills and influence.*

While speaking skills had a significant effect on ratings of influence (63 per cent correlation), which we would expect, listening skills had an effect on its own that was almost as large (54 per cent correlation).

They also found that, for people with good verbal expressiveness, good listening skills had a particularly profound impact on enhancing influence. The researchers suggest this is because listening builds trust. Being good at listening will make you more influential – whether you are good at speaking or not. If you are, its effect is profound.

Silence

'In the silence is the truth.'

Silence is a magic part of conversation. Most people feel a little uncomfortable with silence. So if you can master it and feel comfortable in its presence, you can increase your authority and control the flow of the conversation more effectively.

Silence after I speak

When I finish speaking, if you can remain silent for three seconds you will indicate that you need to think about what I said. That tells me you respect it and signals that I have said something important. Jumping in with a quick response belittles what I have said by telling me you don't need to think about it to respond: my point was obvious and your answer was easy.

And if you give me a silence, I may just try and fill it myself. Since I have said what was easiest to say, the next things I speak may be

*Daniel Ames, Lily Maissen and Joel Brockner, 'The Role of Listening in Interpersonal Influence', *Journal of Research in Personality*, 46, 2012.

deeper, more personal and more revealing. You can learn a lot when your next question is silence.

Silence after you speak

When you have finished saying what you intended to say, what do you do? Do you stop? That is what you should do.

Too often, we feel the need to add something else, to qualify what we have said, or to check 'Was that okay?' When you do that, you are diminishing the power of what you said. It becomes less authoritative and robs me of the chance to really evaluate it.

The bonus that silences offer a speaker is that they slow you down and increase the sense of gravitas and charisma that you broadcast. If you want to speak so people listen, make silence your friend.

Telephone conversations

Follow the same advice for a telephone conversation as you would face-to-face. Here are some of my top tips for applying it.

Speaker's checklist: tips for a telephone conversation

Before making a call

→ Plan your call. What is your desired outcome? How will you open the conversation? What will you do if you go through to an answerphone?

→ Keep a notebook by your phone. Start each call by writing the date and the name of who you are calling, ready to take notes.

→ Turn off your computer or move away from it.

→ As you dial, clear your throat. As it is ringing, smile.

Picking up a call

→ As the phone rings, stop what you are doing and clear your throat.

▶

→ Then answer the incoming call promptly, smiling as you pick up the receiver.

→ Offer a cheerful welcome, then identify yourself clearly.

→ If you know the caller, tell them you are glad they called.

→ Move any food or drink out of reach, to avoid temptation.

→ Keep a notebook and pens by your phone. As soon as you know who is calling, write the date and the name of who it is, ready to take notes.

During the call

→ If you called, start by checking it is a good time to call and how much time the other person has available.

→ Speak slowly and clearly. Be enthusiastic and friendly. Make use of pauses.

→ Use the caller's name.

→ Consider standing up. It will give you more energy and enable you to be more focused with your time.

→ If you sit, sit upright. It will improve your concentration, your voice, and the subtle impression the other person will form.

→ Listen hard – resist temptations to interrupt.

→ Make notes.

→ Offer to spell difficult words. If necessary, use A-alpha, B-bravo, C-charlie to ensure that the other person gets it right.

→ Report back names, numbers and addresses, to check you have them correctly.

→ Stay courteous and respectful … which includes not taking other calls!

Ending the call

→ Summarise the conversation and any agreements.

→ If appropriate, repeat your name, affiliation and contact details.

→ Say goodbye as if you have enjoyed the call and look forward to the next one. Thank them for their time.

→ Don't be the first to hang up, unless you have both agreed that there is nothing more to say.

After the call

→ Review and clarify your notes. Add anything that is missing.

→ Carry out or schedule any follow-up tasks.

GOOD PHONE PRACTICE / BAD PHONE PRACTICE

Bad phone practice

Good phone practice

Speaking with little purpose

Some conversations serve little or no purpose. They make neither party better informed, happier or wiser. They resolve nothing, generate no new ideas, make no progress and do nothing to improve your relationship. They don't even make a pleasant pastime.

If you spot one of these **unproductive conversations**, the best thing you can do is back out of it gracefully and get on with something more useful and pleasant. Let us survey four typical examples, so you can recognise them.

Stifling conversations

Have you ever felt that someone was stifling you? Probably with good intent, but they were holding you back by being over-protective, over-caring and over-bearing. At best, they were protecting you from making your own mistakes; creating a sense of dependency upon them. At worst, they were patronising you; making you feel small and possibly even portraying you that way to others. Subtle though it is, this is the exercise of power by one person over another. It may not feel aggressive, but it is certainly not respectful.

Critical conversations

Some people just know what is right – without a doubt in their minds. Ironically, they often do not have the expertise that could justify such certainty. Instead, they are relying on half-remembered rules and yesterday's experience. But criticising you makes them feel good. At the very best, such critical conversations drive compliance with one person's expectations, denying others any responsibility. At worst, they may be based on outmoded thinking or be blind to the particular realities of the situation. They deny opportunities for finding creative alternatives. This is another way of exerting power and it too can create long-lasting resentment.

Petulant conversations

Stamping of feet and raging against injustice rarely do more than draw attention to the speaker. Arguing without evidence and taking a contrarian stance – often without taking responsibility to act – is mere petulance: an attempt to exert power without any authority. At best, petulant conversations strive for new ideas and new freedoms, but often to little or no effect. At worst, they create pointless dissension and conflict.

Submissive conversations

In some unproductive conversations, the goal is to avoid taking responsibility by compelling another person to accept it. The very best this could achieve is to satisfy a desire for safety, but this is often more illusory than real. More realistically, it destroys not just the respect that people have for you, but your own self-respect too.

Speaker's checklist: ways to turn people off from listening to you

→　Smothering and gently dominating.

→　Criticising, telling and assertively dominating.

→　Complaining, ranting and aggressively dominating.

→ Shouting, yelling and screaming.

→ Whispering, mumbling, using evasive language and avoiding eye-contact.

How to Speak so People Listen

- → Talking too much…
- → … especially about one thing …
- → … which is often yourself.
- → Interrupting and trying to dominate the conversation.
- → Moaning and whinging about things you are unprepared to act upon.

Speaking with real purpose

On the other hand, **mature conversations** have a real impact on the world. They create new thinking, share insights, develop plans and make decisions. They improve relationships, help us to develop, and make people feel good. Mature conversations are characterised by self-respect and mutual respect; respect for facts, evidence and reason; responsibility and willingness for accountability; and by genuine choice in how to respond.

In the last section of this chapter, we will look at three examples of speaking with real purpose:

1 Motivation (not its unproductive cousin, manipulation).
2 Praise (not its unproductive cousin, flattery).
3 Feedback (not its unproductive cousin, criticism).

And in the next chapter, we will focus on some of the hardest conversations of all, **complicated conversations**, which will get more adversarial as we move through Chapter 8:

1 Giving bad news.
2 Relaying tough messages.
3 Arguing.
4 Handling breakdowns in relationships.
5 Dealing with conflict.

Before we look at some examples of speaking with real purpose, let's start with a crucial concept. It will serve us well here and in the next chapter, when we look at complicated conversations. I call it **inner-circle speaking**.

Inner-circle conversations

How we communicate arises in part from having to balance a tension between two needs:

→ Independence from other people.

→ Involvement with other people.

As a result, we often find ourselves hiding our true message – what we truly observe, think and feel – behind a mask of social conventions. These protect us from what we fear: exposure of our true thoughts and feelings. Our need for independence partially obscures our message.

This is **outer-circle speaking**. Not only does it mislead listeners and fail to communicate the truth, but it also has a second effect: it undermines our credibility. This is because, superimposed on top of the message that we are putting out deliberately are a whole set of other messages that are leaking out of us, below our conscious awareness. These **meta-messages** communicate something of our true feelings, and the disparity between them and our deliberate outer-circle speaking.

People notice these differences in our gesture, posture, facial expressions, voice tone and pace, and shifts in pitch and volume, and even through our unconscious choices of words. Examples of this are when we make **Freudian slips**.

People aren't interested in listening to the social conventions of speech: they want to listen to *you* – the real you: your passions, your feelings, your convictions. When your speech is not clouded by conflicting meta-messages that confuse people, people will listen hard. They will also believe you, because you will come across as confident and congruent.

As the Duke of Albany says in Shakespeare's *King Lear*:

'Speak what we feel, not what we ought to say.'

When you say what you are really thinking, and strip away the meta-messages to expose your true self, this is **inner-circle speaking**. This is the route to making complicated conversations successful, and engaging listeners one hundred per cent.

INNER AND OUTER-CIRCLE SPEAKING

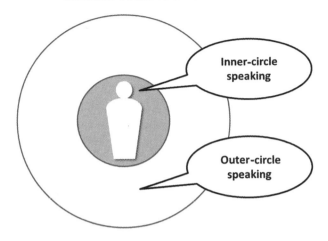

When communicating information is paramount, a conversation can follow four rules, as set out by Paul Grice:*

1 Say as much as you need to; no more.

2 Be honest.

3 Be relevant.

4 Be clear.

Often, however, conversation has other, social, purposes. As a result, we must also add courtesy to Grice's four rules.

From the laboratory: politeness and respect

Politeness and respect are not the same thing. Politeness is a set of meta-messages designed to balance our needs for independence and involvement. Robin Lakoff, a socio-linguist at Harvard University, set out three rules that we can follow, to achieve balance and be polite: ▶

---

*Grice's conversational maxims were first published in 1967. They were reprinted in *Syntax and Semantics*, *Vol. 3*, edited by Peter Cole and Jerry Morgan (Academic Press, 1975).

1 Don't impose on others: maintain a social distance to maintain independence.

2 Offer options so the other person can make a choice.

3 Be friendly, to increase involvement.

Politeness therefore gives us emotional payoffs by creating a defence around ourselves and by building rapport.*

Candour spectrum

Inner-circle speaking creates a challenge for us. We must balance a need for social politeness and all the benefits it confers with a desire for real candour. This creates a spectrum of possible responses between the extremes of being downright blunt and a fear of being honest:

→ **'I say it like it is'**: If you are proud of your no-nonsense bluntness and you make no attempt to see other people's perspectives, this does not recognise the inherent self-centredness of what you are saying.

→ **'No, no – no problem'**: If you are afraid of being honest, you will confine all your speech to the outer circle. It reflects nothing of substance and fails to communicate anything *you* want to say.

True inner-circle speaking is able to respect both yourself and the other person. You are honest, you are open and you speak in a way that respects the other person's integrity.

Motivation (not manipulation)

What motivates someone is as variable as people themselves, so there are many theories of motivation, each offering its own prescription. When you are able to have an inner-circle conversation with someone, you can gain insights into their deeper levels of understanding: their needs and deeper feelings. Here is where our values reside. This is the route to effective motivation.

*Robin Lakoff, 'The Logic of Politeness, or Minding Your P's and Q's', Papers from the Ninth Regional Meeting, Chicago Linguistic Society, 1973.

If you can understand what is important to me, then you can relate what you want me to do to those values, and so motivate me effectively. What these needs are can vary from day to day and from one situation to another, so you also need to be sensitive to who I am today and not make assumptions that what is important to me now is the same as what would have motivated me yesterday.

Avoiding manipulation is a matter of steering clear of the three manipulator's tricks:

Asking you to do something you won't be able to do

If I set you up to fail with a task I know is beyond your capabilities, or if I know you won't have the resources or cooperation you need, then any motivation I offer will be a deception.

Promising you a reward I won't deliver

If I motivate you with a promise I cannot or will not deliver – and I know or suspect this in advance – then my promise is nothing but a lie.

Delivering a reward that you won't value

I may make a promise and deliver, but if I know that the reward has less value to you than the effort you put in, then the bargain was not a fair one: I cheated you.

Praise (not flattery)

Offering sincere praise will not only make you feel good, it will increase your liking of me. So it is vital that I do not try to manipulate you with false flattery, just to win your favour. Most of us find giving sincere praise to be a challenge, so here are my three favourite techniques:

The little stroke

A simple, understated comment of appreciation, applied at the right moment, can remind someone that we value their contribution: 'Nice work' or 'Well done' or just 'Thank you'.

The knee-jerk praise

When somebody does something especially good, allow yourself to show your feelings about it spontaneously. This works especially well in cultures where it is unusual to show how you feel: 'Wow!' or 'Fantastic!' or 'I am *really* impressed'.

The particular favourite

When you look at something I have done and select one particular part to praise, I know that you must have reviewed all of it. Chances are you will pick the part I am proudest of, showing me how much care you have taken. And if you pick a part that surprises me, it can have even more impact: 'I really like …' or 'This bit is excellent' or '… impressed me the most'.

Feedback (not criticism)

Good feedback gives me information that will help me to assess what I have done, make changes if I choose and to perform better next time. Criticism, on the other hand, is all about telling me what you think – which may or may not be helpful as feedback. Three things make feedback particularly valuable:

What you observed

Make sure your feedback is based on behaviour that you have observed. Make it as specific as possible, to help me focus my response precisely, and give me examples and evidence that I can evaluate. Avoid personal comments about me, and concentrate on what I did and how it relates to what I was trying to achieve.

Why it matters

To motivate me, I need the 'because'. So show me the impact of my actions and how that will change if I choose to make changes to how I behave in the future. Also put yourself on the line: why does it matter to you?

Shared responsibility

Feedback needs to be a shared responsibility between me – performing the action – and you – observing it. Therefore the process needs to be an open dialogue, with good-quality listening and questioning from both of us, to help me develop the best possible understanding of the impact of my choices.

The YES/NO of conversations

YES

→ Remember the 'you principle' and focus your conversation on the person you are speaking with.

→ If you want to speak so people listen, learn to listen well yourself …

→ … and make silence your friend.

→ Phone conversations matter – treat them with as much respect as a face-to-face conversation and learn the secrets of doing them well.

→ Use politeness and social conventions to build rapport.

→ Remember that inner-circle conversations communicate powerfully.

NO

→ Don't judge what I am saying while I am speaking – just listen.

→ Don't use 'I say it like it is' or 'No, no – no problem': both are disrespectful – the one of me and the other of yourself.

→ Avoid manipulation, flattery and criticism.

→ Remember that outer-circle conversations remain superficial.

→ Steer clear of unproductive conversations of any sort – stifling, critical, petulant or submissive.

Focus on complicated conversations

Chapter Eight

We all know a complicated conversation as soon as it gets started. In fact, we mostly spot it in advance, which triggers an adversarial or defensive reaction that does nothing but make the conversation more complicated still. We need to understand what makes a conversation complicated and find ways to manage it effectively. As with all things, if you prepare for it and follow a sound process, you give yourself the best chance of success.

Creating complications

Strong emotions are clearly the first element that comes to mind in recognising a complicated conversation. This is usually because we know that there are important consequences to getting it right or wrong. Therefore one particularly strong emotion can dominate: fear. We fear the consequences: succeed or fail.

This also gives us another contributing factor: uncertainty. The high stakes and emotions of a complicated conversation make it hard to predict what will happen. This is compounded by the fact that they are often about complex issues with many inter-woven themes and concerns. Alternatively, they may be far simpler: a polarised disagreement about two different interpretations of reality. This brings us to another common factor: baggage. We each create our own stories about reality by filtering it through our own distinct experiences. We pick up emotional and interpretational baggage along our journeys. This conflicts with other people's baggage.

Speaker's checklist: eight things that can create complications

1 Important consequences

2 Complex issues

3 Uncertainty

4 Strong emotions

5 Fear

Forming stories

We saw in Chapter 2 how we each create our own version of a story by filtering what actually takes place in the real world. Let's examine this process in more detail. The diagram below illustrates the process by which we move from a situation to an action. We will focus on the story-making stages in the middle, so we can understand how we can each form different – and sometimes conflicting – stories.

THE STORY-FORMING PROCESS

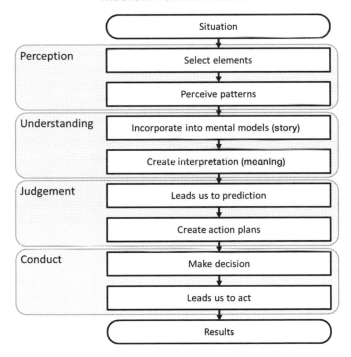

	Situation
Perception	Select elements
	Perceive patterns
Understanding	Incorporate into mental models (story)
	Create interpretation (meaning)
Judgement	Leads us to prediction
	Create action plans
Conduct	Make decision
	Leads us to act
	Results

Perception

The first stage in story-forming is how we perceive the world. When we observe a situation, we inevitably select which **elements** to focus on, meaning others are filtered out and lost to our awareness. This creates a bias.

Then your pattern-forming brain takes the information you have selected and starts to make sense of it by spotting how it conforms to **patterns** you already recognise. There is an element of feedback here, as the familiar patterns can exert a pressure on what information you select, forcing the world to fit in with your prejudices.

Example: Jade's boss asks her to re-do a proposal, putting more emphasis on the company's quality standards. Jade has always felt that her written work is her main weakness, so she interprets this as more evidence of her inadequacy.

Understanding

Now we merge the patterns we perceive into our existing **stories** about ourselves and our world. This will modify our story – but rarely radically. From this, we can build a story about what is happening.

Our great need for **meaning** compels us to see this story in terms of reasons, cause and effect, and intentions. These are not always present in the real, complex and sometimes random world. And when they are, we don't always get them right. Real events don't have an intrinsic meaning. The only meaning they have is that which different observers give them. If you and I each create a different meaning for the same event, then it is no wonder if we conflict over how to act.

Example: Now, in Jade's mind, this brief exchange means that her boss is unhappy with her performance. With summer promotions reviews coming up, she is concerned that she will get overlooked.

Judgement

Once we have a story about events, we can play it forward in our minds to **predict** (accurately or not) what will happen next. Our interpretation of meaning will, of course, influence how the story plays out in our imagination. Our predictions may be flawed by being based on one interpretation of a selective reading of partial information about reality.

Example: Jade now sees that she will either have to work for another year without progressing or start applying for other jobs to move her career on. Unfortunately, she is worried that her poor written work will make her CV and written applications unattractive.

We rarely notice how much our predictions are based on assumptions. And how often do you try out different sets of assumptions to generate multiple future storylines? This process is the basis of **scenario analysis** and is a valuable way to prepare for a complicated conversation. With each prediction, you can start to put yourself into the story to determine what you could do. This gives you a range of options for action. Selecting which **action** you will take will determine the future.

Conduct

We think our decision making is far more logical and reasoned than it really is. Most **decisions** are based on emotions. How we feel about the way our plans play out in our minds dictates which course we choose. Only then do we justify our choice by selecting and interpreting the relevant facts to support our decision.

Example: Jade decides that at lunch she will skip going out with some friends and find somewhere quiet to phone recruitment agencies.

Only now can you **act**. With complicated situations, fear and uncertainty can often hold you back. Sometimes this delay is harmful – other times it is protective. If only we were better at gauging which … but that's another book.

Example: If only Jade had asked her boss why he wanted her to re-do a proposal, putting more emphasis on the company's quality standards. He would have reassured her that the first draft was excellent, but that he had had a call from the client asking for more information on quality, because all suppliers need to meet their own standards.

The tools for a complicated conversation

Inner-circle speaking, which you read about in Chapter 7, is an essential tool for handling a complicated conversation well. It allows you to speak about an honest representation of your reality and invites the other person to do the same.

At the core of a complicated conversation is a joint attempt to build a shared understanding of what is going on. This is not merely about getting at the facts: it is about dealing with the perceptions, interpretations and beliefs that flow from them. At its heart, a complicated conversation is about merging two stories into one.

To support you in this, you have four tools:

1 Inner-circle speaking
2 Deep dialogue
3 Intense attention
4 Future focus

We have examined inner-circle speaking, so now let's look at the others.

Deep dialogue

'Deep dialogue' is my term for a conversation where information flows absolutely freely. Both parties have the courage to examine it, test and challenge it. They must be prepared to review – even overturn – their interpretations of that information. This exchange must not be impeded by euphemisms or unclear language, or by censoring inconvenient truths. The diagram below illustrates the difference between a deep

DEEP AND SHALLOW DIALOGUE

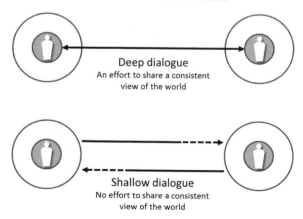

Deep dialogue
An effort to share a consistent
view of the world

Shallow dialogue
No effort to share a consistent
view of the world

dialogue that seeks to merge two stories through inner-circle speaking, and a shallow dialogue that is shrouded by outer-circle speaking and censoring of information.

Intense attention

To work, deep dialogue needs intense listening: opening up your inner circle to receive. Only such intense attention can create the opportunity for a response from your inner circle. Paying such intense attention to another person can transform your relationship. It can evoke a powerful response from you, and the trust it shows will almost certainly be reciprocated.

You can pay intense attention only when you decide that, at this moment and in this place, nothing is more important than this conversation. Become curious, choose to care, and exclude all else. Ten steps to such powerful listening are on page 120.

Future focus

Complicated conversations arise because of either a clash in interpretations or a difference in priorities. Different stories lead to different perspectives on what has happened in the past. These often lead to blame and recrimination. Different priorities arise from what is important to us, now. If you want your complicated conversation to resolve anything, it must at some point move its focus forward, to the future. In the future lie options, and options give choice. Choice gives us control that, in turn, starts to remove some of the stress responses that drive our fear about an uncertain future.

How to manage a complicated conversation

The word 'complicated' literally means 'folded together'. Your purpose in engaging in a complicated conversation is to unfold your two stories so that they can be laid side by side, compared and reconciled. There may still be differences, but you need to understand and respect the differences, even if you choose not to agree.

Seven-step process

These seven steps represent an effective process for conducting a complicated conversation. It does not require that both participants know the steps, as long as you can keep the process on track.

Step 1: What matters?

Step 2: Let's feel safe

Step 3: Truths

Step 4: Invite a deep dialogue

Step 5: Story-telling

Step 6: Share feelings

Step 7: Future thinking

Step 1: What matters?

What do you want? From me, for you, for me and for our relationship? Think about what you want to communicate, what you want to learn, what agreement you want and what actions you would like us to commit to. Also think whether these may be achievable, and at what level you will be content, if you cannot achieve them in full.

And if you know what you want, how do you need to behave, to get it? The biggest challenge is often to control your emotional state.

A great technique for helping you get your thoughts clear in your mind and for slowing down and getting a grip on your emotional responses is the **SCOPE process**.

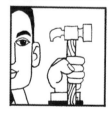

Speaker's toolkit: the SCOPE process

→ **Stop:** Make a mental pause and take a few deep breaths. In a strongly adversarial context this may even mean physically withdrawing from the process for a short time.

→ **Clarify:** What is going on? What do you need to achieve – and what do you want to achieve? What do you know about me and what I want and need to achieve?

How to Speak so People Listen

→ **Options:** What are your options? More options mean more choice. More choice means you have more control. Be creative and generate as many ways you could proceed as possible and then play out the scenarios. Which ones seem to work best and which seem to fail? Make a choice about what you are going to do.

→ **Proceed:** Be determined and courageous, but notice how I am responding and how the situation is evolving.

→ **Evaluate:** How is it going? Constantly evaluate what is happening against your expectations and hopes. Never be afraid to review your approach. If you aren't going in the right direction, return to step 1 and 'stop'.

Step 2: Let's feel safe

Complicated conversations often arise when one or both people feel fear. You will not make any real progress until you both feel safe enough to confront those fears.

We feel safe when we sense mutual respect; so be respectful. Set out a common purpose that you can commit to and that you will ask me to commit to. When I do, I will shift my ground towards a greater level of respect. If you don't receive a respectful response, then carefully point this out.

A common purpose starts you towards rapport. Choosing the right time and place for your complicated conversation is another way of establishing rapport. If I feel inconvenienced by the time or uncomfortable about the place, I will not be willing to engage fully. Another way to invite rapport – which may sometimes be appropriate – is an apology. Use the other techniques you learned in Chapter 7 to strengthen rapport.

The **four Cs** will help the other person feel safe with you:

→ **Confidence:** Like an infant, adults feel safe in the presence of someone who is clearly confident that they know what they are doing. Be confident of the process, of your preparation and of your right to have this conversation. But avoid over-confidence or arrogance, and balance your confidence with a measure of humility.

→ **Control:** You must also be conscious of your feelings – although you need the self-control to choose when to let them show. Be in control of yourself: don't be quick to anger, to take offence, to judge or to interrupt.

→ **Compassion:** Show the other person that you care about them and their feelings, that what is important to them has value, and that you will not be drawn into blame, recrimination or point-scoring.

→ **Collaboration:** Demonstrate your desire to genuinely work together towards a successful complicated conversation. This means you must be open to creating a shared definition of 'successful'.

Step 3: Truths

Now you need to further strengthen your rapport and safety by building a platform of agreement. Look for any objective facts upon which you can both agree. Check your understanding of these facts and build a foundation from which you can proceed with confidence. You may need to start a long way back to find something you can both agree on.

Be honest about your own past actions and behaviours and where they have fallen short of what you each could expect. Acknowledge how your interpretations of the facts differ. Distinguish facts from opinions, and offer up opinions that you have, in the past, treated as truths.

How you feel is a truth: it *is* your emotion. It may be based on a false perception, but the emotion is a real experience. Invite a conversation about how you each feel about the situation and how you got to where you are with it.

Speaker's toolkit: the gemba

Gemba is a Japanese term that means 'actual place'. In Japanese, the phrase 'going to the *gemba*' means heading for where the work is done or where the event happened: the real place. When you want to solve a problem, go to the *gemba* – make it real.

THE GEMBA

現場

Step 4: Invite a deep dialogue

With some agreed truths as a starting place, now invite the other person to share a deep dialogue in which you can explore your respective stories. This is the last stage of building trust and feeling safe.

Speaker's toolkit: appreciative inquiry

The concept of appreciative inquiry (AI) was developed by David Cooperrider as a tool for effecting organisational change. The principle works very well for understanding and changing our own perspectives in a complicated conversation.

The basis of AI is asking questions that focus on finding out what works and how to extend it into problem areas. It starts from what is good and uses it to help imagine how to make bad things good too. From there, you discuss what should be and then move on to planning what will be.

You will see echoes of AI in this seven-step process. Story-telling about things that pleased, excited and involved us is often the first step of AI.

Step 5: Story-telling

Your story first, or theirs? That is a tricky one. If you feel the need to explain, even apologise, telling your story first can create the spirit of openness you need. It gives you the chance to act with the honesty and candour you want.

Speaker's tip: the dangers of hyperbole

Hyperbole is deliberate exaggeration or generalisation for effect. If you do this, using words such as 'always' and 'never', you will only weaken the impact of your words, as well as failing the test of real honesty.

On the other hand, if you both come to this stage equally ready to talk, then inviting the other person to speak first is respectful and declares a willingness to listen and to be affected by their story. Be curious about their story and practise intense attention.

Speaker's tip: the question 'Why?'

Steer clear of the question 'Why?' at this stage. We feel this as a direct challenge to our decisions and therefore to our values. It usually evokes nothing better than a defensive response. If you must know why, try instead asking something along the lines of 'When you ... what were your reasons for your decision?' A question that avoids 'why' and focuses on process or reasoning will be more effective.

Step 6: Share feelings

How do you feel about what you have heard from the other person? Safety and trust need to be at their highest now, because you must each open up your emotional responses to the other and be prepared to understand at these levels too. This means being open to understanding each other's feelings and your own deepest needs and feelings. This will allow you to understand what really matters to the other person. Our feelings are a truth. They are true to us, even if others do not understand or share them.

At this stage in the complicated conversation you will feel yourself under pressure to start resolving the problem, but you are not quite ready yet. Make sure you finish sharing your feelings fully. So if you find yourself wanting to offer a solution, stop.

What matters most now is that you each convincingly demonstrate that you understand the other person's feelings. Allow yourself to reflect back what you are hearing and acknowledge the nature and strength of the emotions they are sharing. Respect their feelings and avoid minimising or criticising them in any way.

Step 7: Future thinking

Only once you have both shared and acknowledged one another's feelings is it time to start thinking about solutions. Moving on to a practical problem-solving footing is often a relief from the more intense emotional conversation.

Often the apparent problem at the start of your complicated conversation will have been big, like a whole pie. Use the listening you have each done to separate off chunks of the pie in which you now understand that there is no problem or that you agree. By gradually reducing the problem down, slice by slice, to the part of the pie that is really at issue, you jointly get a sense of a more realistic scale for the problem: sometimes nothing but a thin slice.

In the sections that follow, we will add to the principles of the seven-step process in some familiar situations.

Speaker's toolkit: a problem-solving process

1 **Name the problem and set objectives for its solution:** Try phrasing the problem *as a* solution: 'How to …'

2 **Determine acceptance criteria:** What will success sound, look and feel like? What standards do you want to apply to your solution to assess if it is good enough?

3 **Gather relevant information:** What are the issues, facts, perceptions and causes that are relevant? Make a dispassionate summary of your stories and feelings. There is rarely 'a singular cause', so look for a cluster of causes.

4 **Create options:** More options equals more choice, equals more flexibility, equals more likelihood of success. Keep asking 'What else could we do?'

5 **Evaluate options:** Use the criteria you determined at step 2 to assess the alternatives you found at step 4, and decide which options are the most likely to succeed.

6 **Test your preferred option:** How do you feel about the preferred option? Notice your reaction and theirs. Comment on your reactions and use them to build on the option and hone it.

7 **Move forward:** Once you know what option to pursue, take the decision, create a plan, put it into action, review progress along the way and evaluate the outcome.

Bad news

Two things can make bad news worse:

→ Pretending it is not bad news, so the other person feels ambushed when they realise it is.

→ Making a big drama out of giving the news, so that the process feels more significant than the news itself.

Nothing will make the bad news better, so the best thing to do is to be quick and efficient about giving it, without being blunt and uncaring. Here are some helpful strategies:

→ It often helps to give a short warning of what is coming, so that the person you are telling can start to prepare themselves. This is also the honest thing to do, because they will probably sense something bad is coming because of your demeanour and often also from the timing and unexpectedness of your approach.

→ Sometimes physically preparing them is important, for their safety. Bad news can literally 'take the legs out from under us', so say 'I have some bad news. Why don't you sit down?'

→ Now, tell them the news directly: 'We are making a number of roles redundant. I am sorry to tell you that your job is one of them.'

→ Give them time to understand what you have said, in silence. Don't try to accelerate this part, it is very important. It may take less than a second or many minutes. Give them time.

→ Be ready to handle strong emotion. With bad news, this is a likely outcome. And give them time to respond as they choose. Listen to their response and avoid criticising it – it is what it is and it is theirs. Respect it. Once again, pause and give them time.

→ It is not respectful to say 'I know how you feel' because you don't. But you can empathise by observing their words and behaviours, and saying something like 'I understand that this must make you feel …'

→ If the response gets too hot, you may need to step away, but the most likely scenario is that it will cool down slowly, with time. If you fear violence, then get out of the way. If you just get anger, avoid confrontational face-to-face postures and too much eye-contact, and allow them to let off some steam.

→ Ask if they want a break or if they want to carry on the conversation. When they are ready, invite questions. When people are in a highly emotional state, their 'rational' brain loses control to their 'emotional' brain, so they need you to take control of the process. This is not the same as taking control of them. Always be respectful in sensing how much control they need you to take.

→ As the conversation comes to an end, offer whatever support you can, and leave them with a simple message about what happens next. It may be the next stage in a process, who to contact for help, when you will speak again or how they can contact you. Keep it simple, because their capacity to process and retain complex information may be compromised by focusing on the news. You may want to write it down for them.

→ If appropriate, check up on them some time later.

Tough messages

Delivering a tough message is much like giving bad news, but without the intensity of emotional response. But there will be emotion, so it is important to break the message into bite-size chunks and listen, with intense attention, between each. Acknowledge any feelings the other person may express.

Because the emotions are likely to be less intense, it can be appropriate to start on some future thinking once you have delivered the message. Help them to think of ways that they can respond to the information you have given them.

Arguing

In Chapter 5 we saw how to spot when an argument becomes a fight, and saw that the purpose of making an argument is to persuade: to achieve agreement. The purpose of two people arguing with one another is also for them to achieve agreement.

We examined the skills to making an effective argument in Chapters 5 and 6. Here, I'd like to highlight a few aspects of how the seven-step process can apply to arguments. Try using it, rather than getting into your habitual argument pattern.

Start by thinking about what truly matters in your argument – is it about being right? It seldom really is, so what agreement do you need and how important is that agreement, set against the importance of your relationship? Find a way to ensure that both of you know that the argument is about finding an agreement and is not personal. This will help you both feel safe to speak from your inner circles, and thus be honest with one another. Share truths and how you feel about them, but crucially separate the objective truths and your feelings into distinct categories.

The deeper your knowledge and the more command you have of the details, the stronger your argument will be. The more you are able to acknowledge and respect the other person's emotional responses, the more effective your argument will be. One without the other – knowledge without respect – will not succeed.

Win or lose, do so with style. If you lose, concede magnanimously. Don't be churlish, because if you are, you won't change a thing but you will miss the chance to strengthen your relationship. The only way to be right all the time is to quickly sense when you are in danger of being wrong and change your stance.

If you win, avoid crowing about it. Again, this will achieve nothing. It is far better to be humble.

Breakdowns

Relationships break down, especially in workplace environments. This could be two colleagues, a boss and staff member, a supplier and customer, or representatives of two organisations working together.

If you want to reverse a breakdown, you need to build back trust and a commitment to working together. What makes breakdowns difficult – and can turn them into conflict, which is discussed in the last section of this chapter – is that rapport has gone. Declaring the breakdown (step 1 below) is important, because it is something both of you can agree on. It is therefore a basis for starting to rebuild rapport.

The process below is one you can drive, one stage at a time, to try and build back your relationship. Although it looks superficially different to the seven-step process for complicated conversations, the two are consistent. The numbers in the diagram indicate which steps each stage corresponds to.

THE BREAKDOWN PROCESS

Declare the breakdown
↓
State your outcomes
↓
Invite my outcomes ① ②

Share the facts ③

State your commitments
↓
Invite my commitments ④

Look for what is missing ⑤ ⑥

Look for options ⑦

Put together a plan

Reiterate your commitment

1 **Declare the breakdown:** You need to state that a breakdown has occurred and what you perceive it to be. Getting this bit right will be the first step in building trust, so talk about why it matters to you. If you did something wrong, say so and apologise. But don't ask for or expect forgiveness or approval. That is not the purpose of this process. *'Last time we spoke, things went wrong ...'*

2 **State your outcomes:** What is the goal you want to work towards? *'What I would like to achieve is ...'*

3 **Invite my outcomes:** Ask me what I want to work towards. I may be content to let the breakdown stand, but this is unlikely. Mending

our relationship will be based on the overlap between your and my desired outcomes. *'What would you like us to achieve?'*

4 **Share the facts:** Be honest about what happened, your own shortcomings, and your emotions. Give examples if they are not obvious to both of you, but avoid blame. Be prepared to acknowledge your different interpretations of events and how you contributed to the problem. Take care to distinguish facts from opinions, and share how you feel about the situation. *'What happened last time was ...'*

5 **State your commitments:** This may include a recap of what you have been committed to in the past, but must focus on what you are committed to now, to help achieve your outcome. *'I am committed to ...'*

6 **Invite my commitments:** Again, be prepared for me to decline to make any at this stage. However, if you do have shared outcomes, and you have got this far, there is probably some rapport and I will probably feel that I do want to offer some commitments of my own, in return for yours. *'What are you committed to, now?'*

7 **Look for what is missing:** There may be missing information – a step in the process, or understanding of how each of us feels – or there may be a gap between our perceptions of what is possible. Steer clear of assuming you know what I intended or was thinking, or offering recriminations. If you do, I will stop being honest with you. *'What was missing for me was ...'*

8 **Look for options:** What are the different ways we could mend the breakdown? If we agree we cannot mend the breakdown, what are our alternatives? Is there a way to deal with things we both need to contribute to, without a good relationship? How? *'Here are some possible ways forward for us ... What ways can you suggest?'*

9 **Put together a plan:** What are the actions, requests, promises, resources and timing that we commit to, to mend our relationship? *'This is what I propose to do ... and this is what I would like from you.'*

10 **Reiterate your commitment:** Explicitly state what you are committed to doing, and then invite me to do likewise. *'I think this plan is a good one, and I am committed to pursuing it as best I can.'*

Conflict

'Speak when you are angry and you will make the best speech you will ever regret.' (Ambrose Bierce)

Conflict tends to arise because we have different values and different choices about what is important. We therefore get into a conflict either to defend our values and beliefs, or to try to persuade others that we are right.

If you do find yourself in conflict, look for ways to manage it in private, because in public you will both feel a need to 'perform' to your audience and will have less chance of listening, hearing, or re-evaluating your position. All you will do is staunchly defend your pitch.

Signs of conflict

When conflict comes, it builds up through a sequence of increasingly powerful negative states, from irritation to anger to abuse to violence. If you can spot the signs of escalation early, you can most easily resolve the conflict before it becomes acute. Body language provides some of the most obvious indicators:

Posture

When we start to feel irritation, we either lean away to ease our discomfort or lean in to signal confrontation.

Gesture

The first gestures betray our doubts or disbelief. Face touching can signal doubt, and blocking our eyes says 'I don't want to see this' – a powerful sign of disagreement. Later gestures relieve the unpleasant feelings of anxiety and insecurity, such as rubbing hands along our thighs or touching our neck by fiddling with a tie or collar (for men) or a necklace or scarf (for women).

Expression

Facial expressions also change, showing the early signs of anger or disgust. Our forehead can start to furrow, indicating the stress we feel from the situation.

SIGNS OF RISING CONFLICT

Defusing the conflict

Defusing conflict needs to proceed through a sequence of increasingly positive states: respect to rapport to collaboration. Rather like the breakdown process, start by making a choice to engage and invite the other person to do likewise. If they do, acknowledge their courage and start to show empathy for their position.

Now air the facts and allow plenty of time to understand each other's viewpoint, concerns and feelings. Agree what criteria you want to set for a suitable resolution, then roll up your sleeves and get to work on some future thinking. When you jointly know how to resolve the situation, agree the steps you will take and make commitments to one another. Nothing (in our culture) beats sealing the agreement with a handshake.

Conflict strategies

You have five basic strategies available to you:

Step away

If the issue is not worth fighting over, then avoid the conflict. Use this either as a permanent solution to pointless issues or as a temporary strategy when either you are insufficiently prepared or when tempers are too hot for real listening to take place.

Make concessions

If winning is not as important as maintaining the relationship, then make the concessions you need to preserve harmony. Allow the other person to feel they have won and show them that there are no hard feelings on your part.

Play to win

On the other hand, if winning really matters – because you are confident you are right and the matter is important to you – then argue your case as strongly as you can. But only do so if you can be satisfied by the outcome – even if your relationship suffers.

Give and take

If the relationship matters and so does winning, then the easiest strategy is to trade concessions so you both feel you have won something. Of course, you have both lost something too, but it will feel fair. Compromise works, but can leave both parties feeling they have given up too much. If you are prepared to invest more effort, there is another way …

Go for a 'win-win'

This is not for every situation, because it needs a lot of trust and takes a lot of effort. It means that rather than trading concessions, you look for what you can do for each other, so you can both take something positive away. Use this strategy when both the matter at hand and the relationship are of great importance to you.

Speaker's checklist: ten conflict management tips

1 Choose the conflicts that are worth engaging with: walk away from the rest.

2 Determine what you want to achieve and what a good outcome will look, sound and feel like.

3 Choose the right strategy.

4 Find common ground – facts and opinions you can agree on – from which to build more agreement.

5 Look for the source of the conflict and address that.

6 The person is rarely the problem. Even if you think they are, don't treat them that way.

7 Practise intense attention and listen more than you speak.

▶

8 Put progress before pride: if you realise you were wrong then say so, say sorry and move on.

9 Flexibility is the secret to success. Keep an eye on your goal and be prepared to try any ideas, from any source, if they might help.

10 Be prepared to credit the other person with resolving the conflict. Recognition is less important than resolution ... and you will always know.

Some people want conflict

For whatever reasons (and they are well outside the scope of this book), some people like to take the opposite view on everything. They enjoy conflict. There is only one strategy for dealing with them: don't engage. You can't win. Your engagement is their win and nothing you do can make you feel better. You will just increase your frustration, anger and bitterness, until you say or do something you will regret. Walk away.

The YES/NO of complicated conversations

YES

→ Know what is most important. Often the relationship will be top. Being 'right' needs to be at the bottom.

→ Get the time and place right – when you have enough time and where you both feel safe.

→ Take responsibility for the process, your actions and your emotions, and keep working to ensure you both feel safe.

→ Check progress as you go. Go back a step or two if you moved on too quickly.

→ Stay in control of your emotional state.

→ Recognise your story is no more 'true' than theirs.

→ Pause for listening and to acknowledge what you heard.

→ Cut up the pie to define clearly where you do and don't disagree.

→ Finish by coming up with a plan for the future.

NO

→ Exaggerating: 'always', 'every', 'never' or 'none'.

→ Using dangerous words: such as 'why' and 'but'.

→ Prejudging: 'You are going to say …'

→ Assuming: 'What you meant was …'

→ Judging: 'You should have …'

→ Blaming: 'This was your fault.'

→ Accusing: 'It was you who …'

→ Criticising: 'You are overreacting.'

→ Overreacting: 'We'll never be able to get past this.'

→ Bringing up dead bodies: 'This is just like last time.'

→ Threatening: 'If you don't …'

→ Sarcasm: 'That's just the way to impress me.'

→ Name calling: 'You are impatient.'

→ Interpreting: 'What you really mean is …'

→ Recommending: 'If I were you …'

Focus on meetings

Chapter Nine

> Meetings are often the way things get resolved, get decided and get done. You spend so much time in meetings that any tips to make that time more effective will be hugely valuable. So we will look at the best ways to make yourself heard and get your point across in this demanding environment – whether you are chairing, participating, networking, selling or persuading.

Meetings are important

The amount of time you spend in meetings will depend on what you do for a living and the social activities you choose. If your work is managerial, you may spend a fifth or even more of your working time in meetings. If you have reached upper management or director level, meetings may be the way much of your work gets done, with half or two-thirds of your time spent in one sort of meeting or another.

If your social life involves organising things such as PTA events, club dinners or charitable fundraising, then these too will involve meetings, as will the many committees we can join, from residents' groups to local political roles. And family life can also be viewed as a series of meetings, at which you and your family all try and influence one another, make decisions and resolve disputes. It seems that modern life is a series of meetings.

Meetings are not just important because they take up so much of your time, but because they are often the places where decisions are taken, information is exchanged, negotiations are conducted, plans are created, sales are made and new ideas are created. You can view a meeting as a conversation, or as a series of conversations for one or more purposes. There are four useful types of meeting, and one that is less so:

Conversation for possibility

This is a discussion to generate new ideas. It is the most creative and freely structured meeting type.

Conversation for opportunity

This is about evaluating ideas and making decisions, so this is where you will need to deploy your persuasion skills to influence others. Sales meetings are a form of conversation for opportunity.

Conversation for action

This is the type of meeting that rolls its sleeves up and gets things done. It solves problems and, once it has a solution, this is where you will make plans, set deadlines and allocate responsibilities.

Conversation for relationships

These meetings are about building and strengthening relationships. Sometimes they achieve little else, but they are also about sharing knowledge and information. When we have a common understanding of reality, this strengthens rapport.

Conversation for ritual

This is a meeting for the sake of having a meeting. Conversations for ritual get little done – not even developing relationships. People attend because they have to, knowing that it will waste their time. So, it should be either cancelled or re-established for a specific purpose.

Meetings are important, because they get things done, but managed poorly, they can waste a lot of time.

From the laboratory: Studer Group research into hospital meetings

The Studer Group is a healthcare consultancy in the United States. In 2006 it published the results of research into meetings in hospitals, which had implications for all organisations. Over a four-week period, three participating hospitals gathered data on the types of meetings that took place, how long they took and how many people attended. Managers and attendees also rated the value and effectiveness of each meeting.

Then managers were given training in how to plan and conduct more effective meetings. After the training, the hospitals collected the same data for four more weeks. The result was a 21 per cent reduction in the number of meetings, resulting in huge financial savings. Both managers and attendees also rated the meetings to be significantly more valuable and more effective.

Chairing

Chairing or facilitating a meeting is an important job, which you must do well if you want to use your time – and other people's time – well. You want people to listen to you, but the irony of chairing a meeting is that the best facilitators say very little. However, it is what they do and how they say the little they do say that has an impact.

We will consider three stages; preparation, conduct and follow-up. For all of them, the most crucial thing is to keep your mind on your purpose. What is the outcome you want to create? And, from that, which of the four useful forms of conversation do you need to facilitate?

Preparation

The first thing to consider is 'What will this meeting be for?' Without a good answer to this question, you have a 'conversation for ritual' and should cancel it. Even with a good reason for meeting, you should ask yourself, 'Do we need to meet?' Is there a better way to deal with the matter than a meeting? You may be able to circulate information, speak to people individually or allocate a task to one or more people.

If you determine that a meeting is worthwhile, then the checklist below will help you to prepare effectively.

Speaker's checklist: preparing for a meeting

Set clear objectives for the meeting

Keep to a few, key objectives. If you need two meetings with the same people, schedule two meetings back-to-back with a break, rather than one long meeting with too many components.

Select, consult and invite participants

Who needs to be there for you to meet your objectives? Don't invite people for the wrong reasons: to avoid hurting their feelings, offending their dignity or because you feel you should. What will they contribute if they attend? Speak to them before finalising an agenda and invitation list. Send invitations in good time for people to prioritise and diarise your meeting.

Plan your agenda

Design a series of conversations that will meet each of your objectives. Think about the sequence, how long each will take and how to facilitate the discussion. Schedule breaks, so that mental fatigue does not impact the meeting's effectiveness.

Identify pre-work

Plan what you and your attendees have to do before the meeting. Put a list of reference materials and requirements on to your agenda, and make it clear that reading and preparing is an important part of the meeting. If you need to, speak with people before the meeting to make sure you have laid the groundwork, but take care not to pre-empt the meeting's decision-making process.

Consider timings, location and facilities

When is the best time for your meeting? If your organisation has a calendar system that allows you to find suitable times automatically, use this. Think about the time of the day and how it fits in with people's other commitments and their energy levels. And decide on where best to hold the meeting. If you have choices, think about the different types of conversation and the room format that will facilitate them. Conversations for opportunity or relationships suggest a less formal environment than a conversation for possibility or for action. You may also need equipment, such as visual aids, flip-charts or communications technology. Finally, will you offer refreshments? No refreshments will help keep the meeting shorter, but offering refreshments will help relax participants. Always have fresh water available.

Distribute your agenda

Produce a written agenda with all this information on it and circulate it early enough for people to do their pre-work. Include supporting materials (or links to them) with it. You can download templates for my 'Agendas for results', based on these ideas, from **www.speaksopeoplelisten.co.uk**

Conduct

Always start on time. So in your agenda make it clear by saying something like 'Start time: 10am sharp'. You could also invite people for 'Refreshments from 9.45 – Meeting starts at 10am sharp'. Not beginning on time will send a signal that late arrival is okay, that the late-comers are more important than the on-timers, and that you are happy to waste the time of the on-timers.

Begin with some social niceties to break the ice and build rapport, even if it is only a couple of minutes. Stating 9.45 for a 10am start will allow time for relationship building without reducing the time for the meeting.

Start the formal business by stressing the meeting's objectives and describing the process (agenda) you plan to follow. From now on, your principal tasks are to encourage useful contributions from everyone and keep discussions on track to meet your objectives.

To do this, there are five primary skills to deploy, each one rooted in the need for flexibility, impartiality and inclusivity.

Invite contributions

Bring people into the conversation, one at a time, determining who should speak and be heard. Ensure everyone's views are heard, paying special attention to those who are least confident and assertive. Ask questions to ensure that the meeting explores all perspectives, and encourage creative and divergent thinking to find multiple solutions to problems.

There can be a tendency for some personalities to dominate and for different points of view to lead to criticism and even personal hostility. It is very much your responsibility to manage and control these behaviours and maintain a positive, equal and respectful atmosphere.

Recognition and praise

A key part of creating a good atmosphere is managing your mental and emotional states and those of your participants. Stay positive and encouraging. Be sure that you know and use people's names. If you don't know everyone in the room, start the meeting with brief introductions and make a note of all of the names on a simple map of the room, which you can keep in front of you throughout the meeting.

How to Speak so People Listen

When people make a contribution, acknowledge it and offer praise for valuable insights, prepared comments and courageous behaviour.

Control the discussion process

Throughout the meeting, ensure everyone is heard and respected, creating an atmosphere where people pay intense attention to each speaker. This will reduce the likelihood of misunderstanding, but if there is any then your role is to ensure that the speaker is able to clarify their point before the conversation moves on.

You must also encourage creative dissension – letting people disagree with one another and make opposing points to fully explore difficult topics. But never let this become a personality clash. In particular, be aware of the power that some participants have, arising from their status, age and experience, knowledge and expertise, connections or sheer personality. These people can dominate a conversation and therefore drive decisions without necessarily being right. It is your job to defuse their power by allowing others to speak and air their points of view fully, before the more powerful contributors prejudice the discussion.

As the meeting progresses, pause to highlight important comments, agreements, decisions, commitments or essential knowledge, to ensure everyone takes note of them. Using a board to record these points ensures a shared view of the meeting's outcomes and acts as a record from which to prepare formal meeting notes afterwards.

Speaker's toolkit: what to do in a meeting that gets out of hand

Here are a number of options that you could try:

→ Stay calm and centred – use the SCOPE process on page 142.

→ Restate the meeting's objectives and the time constraints.

→ Focus on one topic at a time – formally note other topics are being parked.

→ Invite a new voice to be heard.

→ Ask for two minutes of silence – and enforce it.

→ Take a break – with a fixed restart time.

→ Restart the meeting with clear ground rules.

→ Park the contentious item for later consideration – possibly at another meeting.

→ Have a quiet word with one or two key contributors.

→ Apologise for the conduct of the meeting and ask for everyone's help in moving forward in an orderly way (a subtle way of chiding and asking for peer support from others who did not appreciate some people's behaviours).

Close the discussions

Constantly keep one eye on time and one on progress. Your judgement will tell you when the time is ripe for a decision and when to close a discussion and move on. Now is the time for you to contribute, summarising the discussion and either noting the decision the meeting has made, calling for a decision or making one, if you have the authority.

End the meeting

End the meeting with a summary of the key points that have been made and agreed – including dissenting points of view. Then review the commitments that each participant has made. State what will happen next, to follow up the meeting. The **triple-A close** is 'agreements', 'actions and allocations' and 'afterwards': what we agreed, what needs to be done and by whom, and what happens next.

Speaker's toolkit: facilitation process

→ **Start a meeting by establishing the ideal outcome and the criteria for success:** This can come from the facilitator or be the result of a conversation among participants.

→ **Establish a clear agenda:** Everyone needs to know the process you will follow and how it fits the meeting's objectives.

→ **Ensure everyone has a chance to comment:** Especially those quiet people who have lots of ideas but are less pushy about sharing them. Often their perspectives can be particularly valuable.

→ **Put or seek counter-views:** Test the robustness of any evidence that is presented and arguments that are made.

→ **End with a triple-A close:** Review agreements, actions and allocations, and afterwards.

Follow-up

Follow up on your meeting by issuing a written summary of commitments and next steps, and by carrying out your own allocated actions assiduously. If it is your responsibility, also ensure that others meet their commitments.

Participating

The first rule of meetings is don't be a 'meeting tart' and attend lots of meetings just because you can.

Pick your meetings and decline invitations where you have little or nothing to contribute to or learn from the meeting. It is also worth looking at the agenda and contacting the chair if you want to attend just one part of the meeting. Agreeing you will arrive partway through or step out after a particular topic can optimise use of your time. I also recommend not accepting any meeting invitation without a clear agenda.

Arrive on time, ready to participate enthusiastically. Whether you want to be there or not, you are there, so put on your game face and act as if it is the most valuable things you could be doing.

Listen well and take notes when others are speaking, and structure your contribution when it is your turn. The structured response frameworks in Chapter 5 (page 65) will help you to make your contributions effective and encourage people to listen when you speak.

Newton's third law of motion is that 'every action has an equal and opposite reaction'. When you tell the meeting something, someone may react and that will create resistance. The reaction to a question, however, is an answer. Questions evoke awareness and are a great way to get the meeting to listen to you.

Speaker's toolkit: remembering names

Whether you are chairing or not, drawing a map of who is where in the room will help you remember names – and if you are not chairing and don't know everyone, it is perfectly reasonable to ask the chair for a round of introductions at the start. If you want to go one step further and memorise the names:

→ You only remember what matters, so pay attention when the name is said.

→ Notice the name: what is unusual? How is it spelt? Mentally repeat it.

→ Practise it – in a meeting, either use it when you introduce yourself or write it down.

→ Mentally – or maybe out loud – remark on the name: where it is from, an unusual spelling or any story that you can create.

→ Link the name to someone or something in your life. The more outrageous the better, but keep this inside your head!

→ Use the name during the meeting – but not too much.

→ Then use it again when you say goodbye.

Shut up

Speak when you have something *valuable* to say, otherwise … shut up. When speaking so that people listen, less is more. What will make your contribution particularly valuable will be if you:

→ contribute ideas;

→ clarify complexity;

→ suggest a process;

→ prompt a decision;

→ help resolve conflict.

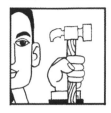

Speaker's toolkit: what to do if you meet resistance

→ Always respect the person who is resisting.

→ Get the resistance out into the open, where you can deal with it.

→ Assume the resister is motivated by a positive reason to resolve an issue. If their behaviour is bad, ask the chair and the meeting to help address that.

→ Avoid mind reading and assuming you know what the source of the resistance is. Be curious and ask questions before you attempt to deal with it.

→ Build rapport by finding out what you can agree on before tackling your differences.

→ Be curious, and find out what you can learn from the resister. There is a chance that they know something you don't.

→ Use the SCOPE process to avoid an emotional knee-jerk response.

You can learn more about handling resistance positively in my book, *The Handling Resistance Pocketbook*.

Networking

Most of the information you need for networking was covered in Chapters 3 and 7. But networking meetings are a special environment, where people often make a few basic mistakes, such as:

Mistake 1: Standing in the corner, waiting for an approach

This won't allow you to meet the people you choose and will give you less time to speak with people. Confidently approach people and enquire politely if they would like to tell you about themselves. Who wouldn't?

Mistake 2: Aiming high

Yes, the chief executive of a global company would be a great contact, but so will the eager young starters in their first job. They will grow and develop and so will their careers. Everyone is worth talking to; you don't know what they will be doing in five or ten years' time.

Mistake 3: Eating when you are trying to communicate

If you want to focus on the networking, then eat beforehand, so you don't go into the meeting hungry.

Mistake 4: Focusing on yourself

The best networkers go in with an attitude of curiosity and set out to learn as much as they can about the people they meet.

Mistake 5: Looking for what you can get from the people you meet

The better approach is to listen for what you can offer them. Let the powers of familiarity and reciprocation work their wonders and soon you will start to receive.

Mistake 6: Failing to follow up on a conversation

Always make a note of any commitments you make or requests they make – and deal with them promptly and efficiently at your next opportunity. Send a note to everyone you met, thanking them for an interesting conversation and offering to stay in touch. If you use social media such as LinkedIn or Facebook, consider inviting them to link with you.

Selling

The six-step process for a sales pitch in Chapter 5 (page 79) will give you the structure you need for a sales conversation. Here, as everywhere else, practise paying intense attention to your prospective customer. They want you to address their needs and you can only do that when you understand them fully. They will only accept your proposal if they believe you understand them fully.

Being believed

How do you get people to believe what you are saying in an environment where there may be some doubts? You may be briefing staff on contentious changes, delivering unwanted news to a local pressure group or even acting as a witness in a legal case.

To increase your chances of being believed – assuming what you have to say is believable – you need to focus on three fundamentals:

→ Attitude

→ Body language

→ Process

Attitude

Getting your attitude right is about balance; balance between confidence in what you are saying and arrogance that nobody could disbelieve you. It is also about the balance between politeness and coming across as submissive. The secret here is the simple courtesy that flows from respecting everyone present – including those who would challenge your point of view.

Body language

The balance your attitude needs to strike must be reflected in your body language, starting with your clothing. Be well dressed for the context you are in but not slick or flashy in any way. Anything inappropriate will undermine your authority.

Face forward and keep your body upright, with a relaxed but alert posture that does not lean to one side. Keep your head upright too. Keep your arms to your sides if standing, or resting on chair arms if sitting. If there are no chair arms, rest them gently on the table, one each side and, if there is no table, rest one hand on the other on your lap. Keep as still as you can, resisting the temptation to fidget with your hands, tap with your foot or shake your leg. Rightly or not, people associate shifting in your seat or on your feet with being 'shifty'. Finally, maintain eye-contact. You may know that this is a poor indicator of truth or lying, but people often don't and will associate a shifting gaze with a shifty person, and avoiding eye-contact with avoiding the truth.

Process

There are seven steps for answering questions so that your answer will sound more believable. You can strip out step 1 and adapt steps 2, 4 and 7, if you are speaking unprompted.

Step 1: Listen carefully to the question, without interrupting.

Step 2: Pause before you answer – even if you know instantly what you want to say. Use the time to think and structure how you answer, and let the silence demonstrate how seriously you take the question.

Step 3: Pace – breathe slowly and speak slowly. Deliberate control of your pace will allow you to slow down, add emphasis where you choose and let your voice settle to the lower end of its tonal register. Speaking too quickly comes across as a sign of nervousness, and high-pitched voices are less trusted than deeper ones.

Step 4: Answer the question and not anything else. Speak to the point, without being abrupt. Use simple language and no jargon or 'clever' words that will arouse suspicion that you are hiding the truth behind sophisticated language. Don't try to explain your thought process. It may be very logical, but it will sound to listeners as if you need to reassure yourself that what you are saying is true, which will diminish your credibility.

Step 5: Address the person who is chairing or facilitating the discussion, the person in authority or, if there are neither, the person who most needs convincing. Turn your whole body towards them and make eye-contact.

Step 6: Facts – don't express opinions or speculate, just offer the facts. Don't guess what you don't know, don't volunteer information that you are not asked for and don't explain your thought process.

Step 7: Stop – when you have spoken your answer then stop. Say no more until asked another question.

Speaker's checklist: tips for sounding truthful

→ Avoid words such as 'honestly', 'truly' or 'candidly'. They weaken the perception of your own confidence in what you are saying.

→ If you are interrupted, let the interrupter finish before you speak again. Then, courteously state that you had not finished, that you will address their point shortly (if you intend to), recap where you had got to, then finish what you planned to say.

→ Answer the question that is asked, not what you thought it should have been. If you are in any doubt, clarify the question before answering.

→ If you are asked about any written material, always read it before giving an answer. Never assume it says what you think it says. It may be a trick or your memory may be faulty.

→ If you get multiple questions, separate them out, list them and tackle them one at a time, verbally ticking them off as you answer each one. Unless, that is, you want to adopt the 'politician's approach' and only answer the ones that you wish to answer.

The YES/NO of meetings

YES

→ Decide what sort of meeting you need and what your objectives are.

→ Start your meetings on time.

→ Use the 'triple-A close' for meetings.

→ Listen – think – speak.

→ Use a clear structure for your answer.

→ Be believed with attitude, body language and process.

NO

→ Don't speak – think – listen.

→ Don't speak unless you have something valuable to contribute.

→ Avoid holding too many meetings – cut out conversations for ritual and poorly managed meetings.

→ Don't be a 'meeting tart'.

→ Avoid the 'six mistakes of networking'.

Focus on
public
speaking

Chapter Ten

It is a cliché that most of us would rather be the subject of a eulogy than the person giving it. It is not true, but it is true that few people have both a real talent for speaking to an audience and the confidence to do it. Yet those who do appear to have a talent use a range of techniques that anyone can follow, to become confident, capable and influential when speaking in public.

This chapter is for anyone who needs to speak in front of an audience, whether at a sales meeting, a professional business presentation or an after-dinner speech. It will show you the techniques that speakers have honed and used over many centuries to ensure that their audiences listen.

The five parts of speaking

The great Roman orators divided the art of speaking, or **rhetoric**, into five parts. A properly trained speaker throughout the Roman era and later ages was expected to master all five of these. They have dropped out of formal education over the last couple of hundred years, but are still very much the basis of writing and delivering great speeches and presentations.

1 Invention
2 Arrangement
3 Style
4 Memory
5 Delivery

Invention

Invention is about creating the story you want to tell: finding the information, thinking about what you want to say, and really getting your ideas clear in your mind. This was, to a large extent, the subject of Chapter 3.

Speaker's toolkit: defusing the BOMB

Before you even start to write your speech, talk or presentation, defuse the BOMB. If you don't have good answers to these four elements, you risk getting it wrong.

Benefit

Who will be in your audience and why should they listen to you? If they will give you their time and attention, what will you give your audience in return?

Outcomes

What do you want to get out of your talk or presentation? How do you want to change your audience's thinking, what do you want them to remember and what do you want them to do as a result of listening to you? Why are you speaking and what would be a great result?

Map

What is the story you need to tell and what are the key messages you want to get across? These will feed into the arrangement phase (below). In Chapter 5, you met the three secrets of persuasive argument: ethos, logos and pathos. How will you use these to make your case?

Background

Do your homework. Who will be in your audience and what will they know? What will their attitudes and expectations be? What information do you need to have at hand to build the detail of your speech or presentation and what additional information will you want to have in reserve to help deal with questions and challenges? There is an old rule: 'Never present more than 20 per cent of what you know.' That way, you will always have plenty of depth.

Arrangement

Next, you need to structure your talk or presentation to create maximum effect: to make it compelling, persuasive and powerful. We looked at this extensively in Chapter 5, starting with the classical approach that the Roman orators would have been familiar with: introduction, narration, division, proof, refutation and conclusion. We do not need to revisit this here.

Style

We have not yet spoken of style: the way that great speakers make it a pleasure to listen to them. This may seem like something of a dark art of professional speechwriters and playwrights, but all they have done is learned, practised and perfected the use of some simple, practical rules of language, which you can learn too.

Memory

There are three reasons why memory is important to a speaker:

1 So that you can memorise **what you are going to say**. Speaking without notes narrows the emotional space between you and your audience, it creates more spontaneity and naturalness – and therefore increases your impact.

2 So that you have a **store of ideas** and snippets that you can contribute to your speech to fill it with interesting asides, thoughtful insights and inspiring quotations.

3 So that you can make your speech **stick in the memories of your audience**. We examined this aspect of memory in Chapter 6, but I will offer you an extra technique in this chapter.

Delivery

The last phase is how you deliver your speech, talk or presentation. In classical times, orators would practise each hand gesture, knowing that their audience would recognise a separate, parallel language in particular arm movements. Even today, the manner of your speech and the effect of your gestures and body language will contribute a lot to how people perceive what you are saying and how much they will want to listen to you.

Style

If you can make your speech a pleasure to listen to it will be one of your greatest talents. I have ten tips to offer you, to help make your style compelling, persuasive and powerful. As you start to build these into your speech, it will grow in impact.

Compelling style

1 Simple

Keep your language clear and easy to understand. Brief is better, and avoid unconventional uses of words or phrases that might jar with your audience.

2 Structure

Create a compelling sequence that is easy to follow and leads your audience to want to hear what is next. Signpost what is coming up, to help them to assimilate each section easily.

3 Surprise

A little surprise here and there will rekindle flagging attention and delight your audience. You can create this using misdirection, unexpected information or a dramatic image or metaphor, for example.

4 Suitable

Please don't over-step propriety in trying to be surprising. Be aware of the occasion and suit your style and content to that. A best man's speech should be different at the wedding reception from what is said at the stag event; a presentation to customers will differ from an in-house presentation to a sales team; and an informative talk about the environment will be different from a political speech on the same subject.

Persuasive style

5 Solid

You must convey ethos with real examples and evidence that is relevant to your audience and demonstrates your personal credibility.

6 Sound

Your logic must be sound, using reasoned arguments arising from demonstrable facts to create a case that your audience will find plausible.

7 Sentiment

Convey pathos by appealing to sentiment at the right time. Real-life examples and the human implications are the best way, but you can also consider talking honestly about yourself.

Powerful style

8 Stories

Stories don't just convey pathos through visceral emotion, conjuring empathy and inspiration; they can also hold an audience spellbound, waiting for the next twist. Nothing is more powerful than a good story well told.

9 Shrewd

Offer your audience astute, penetrating and wise insights into your topic, so that they really want to hear your thoughts on your subject.

10 Stylish

Ornament your speech with some of the flowers of rhetoric: the clever ways that speakers have found to create patterns from words that entrance and delight listeners.

Speaker's toolkit: rhetorical techniques

There are a great number of big academic texts, covering well over 400 rhetorical figures of speech that use language to create a pleasing or intriguing effect for the listener. And this is not the place to add another one. Even a sampling of the more common techniques is a tricky task. So rather than offer an orderly checklist, here are a few personal favourites, grouped under headings that should make it easy to remember the essential ideas behind them.

Making music with words

Rhythm, rhyme and repetition grab our attention, and when the first sound in each word is the same, we call it **alliteration**. Commonplace sounds are well-represented by words, such as 'screech' and 'moo'. If you can invent new sound-words (called **onomatopoeia**) you will attract attention.

Patterns of repetition

There are so many patterns to choose from, starting with the most basic: 'Yes, yes, yes' (called **epizeuxis**). My favourites are:

→ Starting phrases with the same word or words: 'This royal throne of kings; this sceptred isle' (**anaphora**).

→ Ending phrases with the same word or words: 'When I was a child, I spoke as a child' (**epistrophe**).

→ Ending one phrase and starting the next with the same word or words: 'Fear leads to anger; anger leads to hate' (**anadiplosis**).

Contradiction and contrast

These are some of the most widely used patterns, from 'It is better to give than to receive' to 'One small step for a man, one giant leap for mankind'. John F. Kennedy – a brilliant speaker – combined this with repetition when he said 'Ask not what your country can do for you, ask what you can do for your country'.

Amplifying or diminishing

Deliberate understatement – such as describing losing a limb as a flesh wound – or deliberate overstatement – like saying of a scratch 'I am mortally injured' – are established ways of drawing attention to something and also highlighting your attitude to it, often in a humorous way.

One thing in terms of another

Poets use metaphor and simile to describe one thing as another, or as being like another, to create a powerfully vivid imaginative effect. When you do it to explain something, this is an analogy. You can also describe things in terms of their components, like when you refer to your car as your 'wheels'.

Messing with sentence structure

The most widely used deliberate effect is to structure a sentence into three parts: 'I came, I saw, I conquered.' Lists of three things have enormous power because of the rhythm they create, and the sense of completion they foster.

Memory

You will recall, I hope, that memory is important to you as a speaker for three reasons: to memorise what you want to say; to remember useful things to put into your talks; and to help you design a presentation that will stick in the minds of your audience.

Remembering your talk

There is a simple method that orators have used to remember speeches for thousands of years. All you need, to make it work for you, is a familiar building or route. Let's say, for example, that you want to use your kitchen, and your speech has seven key points in it that you want to remember.

Imagine you are standing at the threshold of your kitchen, looking in. Start to your immediate left and sweep your eyes around the room slowly, from left to right, noticing things like windows, the sink, the cooker, the fridge, a table, a kettle, a toaster. Identify seven things that tend to stay where they are, so that you have seven hooks, in a sequence, which you will not forget.

Now start with the first key point in your speech. Perhaps, in your introduction, you want to remember to talk about the impact of last winter's bad weather on sales. Your first hook is a window, so in your mind conjure up a vivid scene of snow drifts and blizzards through your window. The more powerful the image, the better. As you picture it, let yourself shiver for a moment: engaging multiple senses aids memory.

The next thing you wanted to talk about was the stockpiles of paper in your warehouse. Your next hook is the sink: imagine a pile of paper in your sink. Picture rolls of paper sticking out, loose sheets overflowing and the plug hole blocked. Make the image startling and comical for maximum recall-ability.

Then move on to the next point you want to make: how you have a plan to save this year's profitability. This will get hooked to your cooker, so picture yourself, the hero, dressed in a superhero costume, saving a crumbling cake from the oven and pulling it out to see it stuffed with £20 notes.

You should now be getting the picture. This is called the **Roman room method** or, more technically, the **method of loci** (the word 'loci' simply means points). Because you are familiar with your room, or a route you travel frequently, remembering that part, in sequence, takes no effort. Vivid images – particularly if they are comical or rude – are easily recalled. By pegging the images to the landmarks in your room or on your route, you can easily commit a long sequence of memory points to your long-term memory with little effort. Reviewing the sequence a few times will make it easy to mentally scan to the next point and see the vivid image, causing you to recall the next point to make.

Mind maps

Mind maps have been around for centuries, but were popularised (and the term protected commercially) by Tony Buzan in the 1970s. These are a way of mapping out a set of ideas in a graphical way and are useful for speakers both to develop their content and sequence, and then to memorise it. However, the memorisation part works in a very similar way to the Roman room method; using images pegged to places on a map. If you are not familiar with mind maps, they offer a new way of note-taking, creative thinking and assisting memory that will be worth investigating. Buzan's books are still the best on the subject.

From the laboratory: the science of memory

You can think of your memory as working in three stages:

Stage 1: *Register* the information

Lots of memory goes wrong here – it falls at the first hurdle. Stuff goes 'in one ear and out the other'. To register it you have to get the information to stop in the middle! So to help you, when you get new information, do something with it: in your mind, comment on it. Make a link between it and something else you know – repeat to yourself.

We have two distinct memory processes: long-term and short-term memory. Your short-term memory can drop an idea in seconds, so remarking on the idea – stopping it on its way back out of your head – gives you the time to move to the next step.

Stage 2: *Retain* the information

This is the step where you transfer information into your long-term memory. We do it by rehearsing the information: cycling it through our short-term memory enough times to cause the chemical changes necessary to create a long-term memory. There are two main processes of rehearsal:

1 The **phonological loop** – the repetition of words.

2 The **visuo-spatial sketch pad** – the creation of images and imagined objects, and using sounds, smells and your other senses.

There are two main types of long-term memory:

1 **Knowing that** – called your **declarative memory**. The two principal forms are **semantic** (ideas and knowledge) and **episodic** (things we experience) memory.

2 **Knowing how** – called your **procedural memory**.

Stage 3: *Retrieve* the information

There are two primary forms of retrieval: recall and recognition. Could you remember the name of the star of the movie *Gladiator*?

If you can, that is **recall**. If you cannot, but remember it as soon as I tell you it was Russell Crowe, that's **recognition**. The trick is to move from recognition to recall by using the memory techniques to help you.

HOW MEMORY WORKS

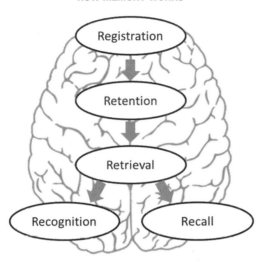

Storing useful information

One way to start a talk is with a pithy quote, or perhaps a reference to an unusual event from the news, or possibly a description of some interesting research you read about in a magazine. But how will you remember these things and have them available when you are writing your talk?

For hundreds of years, people who need to speak publicly have been storing up these useful snippets in notebooks, known as **commonplace books**. Many famous people have even published theirs, giving us all access to the witty remarks and fascinating snippets recorded by people in public life. You can keep one too, by keeping a simple notebook with you at all times.

And if you are a more high-tech sort of person, why not use one of the many note-taking apps available for smartphones? Some of them easily share information across all your devices, making it straightforward to copy-and-paste the quote from your notes app to your presentation notes.

Helping your audience to remember

We covered this in Chapter 6, but I'd like to offer you one more specific extra technique, which is a great tool for speakers: the **memory anchor**.

We know that vivid images, smells, sounds and other sensory information are more easily remembered than abstract facts. If you can link a fact, idea or piece of information to some vivid stimulus, you can create a deliberate anchor in the minds of your audience. Whenever they are exposed to that stimulus again, the act of recall will bring back with it the idea that you attached to it.

So, for example, if you want your audience to remember a powerful sales slogan, then exposing them to it alongside a vivid image, with a strong dominant colour and a distinctive tune, will cause them to anchor the slogan to the image and sound. Replaying the sound with the image will trigger recall of the slogan. Making the image easy to recall on its own will bring back the slogan with it.

In case you are wondering if this works, this is precisely how a large number of adverts are designed to work. More **hidden persuaders**!

Delivery

Delivery is a big topic. So I have divided it into three sections:

1 Preparation

2 Speaking

3 Handling questions and challenges

Preparation

We are nearly ready to think about your big moment: delivering your speech, talk or presentation. But not quite yet: first, you need to prepare. There are three things we need to cover: rehearsal, mental preparation and physical preparation.

Rehearsal

The amount of rehearsal you need to do is a personal matter, but if your talk really matters, then do more than you think you need to. Ironically, the shorter your talk, the more rehearsals you will need to do, to get your comments sharp and pithy.

If you have a presentation that matters a lot and you are not an experienced speaker, then it will be well worth working with a good friend or colleague to act as a rehearsal buddy or coach. If you can, also rehearse with a friendly audience. At least four (ideally seven) run-throughs will prepare you well. Here is a seven-step routine. If you are pressed for time, drop steps 2, 5 and 7.

1 Run through your notes, on your own, to start to learn the content. You may need to do this a few times. Improve your recall by testing yourself.

2 Run through the talk on your own, with no notes. This will help you to consolidate your memory and spot where you need to focus.

3 Run through your speech with an observer or coach. Ask them to give you three points for you to focus on to improve your performance.

4 Have another run-through with an observer or coach – working on your three points. Ask them to give you feedback on the changes and to offer three more points.

5 Repeat as often as you have time for.

6 Have a run-through with a friendly audience to simulate interaction. This 'dress rehearsal' should give you confidence. Get comments.

7 Final run-through with audience. This is all about confidence. If you must get feedback, ask for one thing only to focus on.

Mental preparation

Mental preparation is about dealing with nerves. Many people get nervous when they think about the prospect of speaking in front of an audience. What you need to distinguish is the difference between:

→ friendly nerves, which get your adrenalin pumping and raise your alertness, so you can do a great job;

→ crippling nerves, which send your stress levels sky high and leave you panicked and fearful.

An example

Jack and Jill were waiting in the wings to speak at their company's annual conference. Jack said to Jill: 'I'm terrified. My heart is racing, I'm sweating all over, my hands are shaking and I just know I am going to make a real mess of this.' Jill replied: 'I know what you mean. My heart is beating so hard I can feel it, I am hot and bothered and my legs feel wobbly. I just know that I am pumped up and ready to go on stage.'

Having nerves is not a problem: it is how you interpret them. There are six processes that will calm you and put you in control of those nerves.

Acknowledge and confront your nerves

You are nervous. Pretending otherwise won't accomplish anything, so acknowledge it. When you do that, it will rob the fear of its power. Notice what a good thing your nerves are: they tell you that this is important and you are taking it seriously.

Believe in yourself

You have invested a lot of time and effort getting to where you are. Mentally check through all the positive things you have done to prepare, from research, thinking and your experiences to date, to the work you did designing your talk and rehearsing it. One trick that works for me is to remind myself that if I miss something out or don't explain something with the nice turn of phrase I have prepared, then I will know

– but no one else will. My audience will judge what I do and say, not what I don't do or forget to say.

Relax

The simplest way to relax yourself is a few deep breaths. Sit or stand upright with a good posture and take six really deep breaths, exhaling as much air as you can between each. Not only do deep breaths send signals to your brain that damp down the release of stress hormones, but they also put a larger supply of fresh oxygen into your blood. This will help your brain work more effectively, making your responses to your audience more resourceful.

If you have long-term stress or stage-fright problems, try learning and practising a meditation technique, such as transcendental meditation or yoga. This will have huge and lasting relaxation benefits. You can find out more about this in my book *Brilliant Stress Management*.

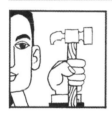

Speaker's toolkit: calming breathing

Stand up and take six deep breaths. Each time, inhale as deeply as you comfortably can and exhale slowly. Make each cycle last longer than the previous one. Each time you breathe out, feel your shoulder muscles relax.

Self-talk

We all talk to ourselves. The question is, what do you say? If you are beating yourself up about gaps in your preparation, worrying about possible pratfalls or reminding yourself about past bad experiences, none of that will help you in any way.

If, on the other hand, you remind yourself about all the preparation you have done, all the past successes you have had and all the ways it can go well, you will help calm your nerves and prepare yourself to succeed. Be your own best friend and coach: talk to yourself as your best friends would talk to you.

Visualisation

Visualisation is an under-used resource. Our minds don't distinguish well between reality and fantasy. So prepare yourself by visualising yourself going on stage, fully prepared, and delivering a first-class presentation or speech. See it in vivid Technicolor. Notice little details, such as how confident you are feeling and how the people in the front row are smiling and nodding when you make your points. Hear yourself speaking clearly and fluently.

Rehearse like this two or three times and, when you approach the stage for real, your unconscious mind will associate good, positive feelings with the experience, and you will start to feel more confident.

Posture

Although posture might be part of physical preparation, the underlying process is mental. Getting your posture right can come most easily from visualising. Stand upright, lightly on your feet, imagining a puppet string attached to your head, pulling you gently upwards. Relax your shoulders, imagining the muscles of your arms melting like chocolate to drip off your fingers.

Now imagine that there is a bubble around you. Imagine it growing and extending outwards, filled with your energy. Keep your mind on the centre of your body, just below your navel, and imagine it solid and unshakeable. These steps will calm and centre you.

Now to boost your energy and confidence. If you want to feel happier and more enthusiastic, gently look upwards, turning your head to the ceiling. As you do, allow your mouth to widen into a broad smile. Hold this posture for 30 seconds. Then repeat.

If you want to feel more confident and assertive, widen your stance, so your legs are slightly wider than shoulder width apart. Now put your hands on your hips, with your elbows outwards. Pull your shoulders back and allow your jaw to come forward a little bit. Hold this posture for 30 seconds. Then repeat.

From the laboratory: the neuroscience of panic attacks

When your hands shake and you start to feel faint, you may be having a panic attack. Don't worry: nothing bad will happen – it is just your sympathetic nervous system going into overdrive. Along with a release of 20 to 30 hormones, your amygdala – the fear centre of your brain – is becoming over-active. Other brain areas also kick in – including a part of your mid-brain called the periaqueductal grey. This region prompts reactions such as freezing or running away, two of the most common responses in speakers who fear the stage.

You can calm this by noticing and acknowledging it, describing to yourself how you are feeling, deep breathing, and positive 'I'm okay' self-talk.

Physical preparation

Physical preparation is about making sure everything is ready, so here are some checklists you can use.

Speaker's checklist: what to pack

→ **Travel documents:** tickets, reservations, ID, maps.

→ **Equipment:** laptop, projector, power leads, timer or watch, music player and music.

→ **Accessories:** remote control, pointer, adaptors for foreign sockets, extension leads, connection cables.

→ **Stationery:** pens, notepaper, pencils, marker pens.

→ **Personal items:** phone (and charger), business cards, purse/wallet, umbrella.

→ **Materials:** your notes, printed materials, reference documents, props.

→ **Backups:** USB or SD drive, login details for cloud backup.

→ **Vanity items:** make-up, tissues, comb, breath mints.

→ **For emergencies:** masking tape, gaffer tape, penknife, sticky notes, plain paper, sticky tac, scissors, painkillers.

You can download a checklist to print and use at **www.speaksopeoplelisten.co.uk**

Speaker's checklist: checks to make on arrival

→ **Visual technology:** Does it work? Run through everything. Are laptops running on power? Are screen savers or alerts disabled?

→ **Audio technology:** Test the microphones, check you have spare batteries.

→ **Sight-lines:** Are chairs well placed? Where will you stand? How clear are visual aids?

→ **Supporting materials:** Have participants got all the materials they need?

→ **Small equipment:** Check you have what you need – such as marker pens, pointers, notepaper and pen, watch or timer.

→ **Comfort:** Ensure there is water (not fizzy and not iced if you are speaking) and tissues to hand.

→ **Distractions:** Empty your pockets, remove dangly bracelets, put away unnecessary potential distractions.

You can download a checklist to print and use at **www.speaksopeoplelisten.co.uk**

One thing not to forget is your appearance. For many people, taking care of their appearance is a part of a routine that helps calm them and make them feel more confident. Dressing well will often boost your sense of self-esteem and presence, so aim to dress a little better than you expect your audience to dress. Make sure that your clothes and shoes are comfortable, so that they do not distract you, and ensure that no aspect of your appearance (typically ties, cufflinks and flies for men, earrings, necklaces and décolletage for women) grabs more attention than your words. My top tip is to pop to the cloakroom just before you are due to start, to make yourself comfortable and to use the mirrors for one last chance to get your clothes straight.

Speaking

pep (noun): energy, high spirits, vitality, vigour
PEP (acronym): passion, energy, poise

Good delivery has PEP. In front of an audience, you need to demonstrate your **passion** and commitment for your subject, **energy** and enthusiasm in your delivery, and **poise** in the way you carry your body and words.

This is vital because your emotional cues don't just leak out, betraying the way you feel about your story, your audience and your presence in front of them: they gush out. One way or another, consciously or not, this is the message your audience will take from your speaking. PEP ensures they focus on the message you *intend*.

This section is about how to put PEP into your delivery. If you forget all the guidance that I gave you in Chapter 5, about drafting a compelling, persuasive and powerful talk or presentation, or the six steps of classical speech-building, remember this: every talk has a beginning, a middle and an end.

Beginning: opening

Your opening is where you grab your audience's attention. Here is where they decide whether to listen to you. If they decide 'yes', there is still plenty of scope to lose them later on but, if they decide 'no' at this early stage, it is very hard to ever regain their attention.

A punchy opening line can seize the initiative from your audience, but many of them need a little time to settle in and feel comfortable. You have a few minutes during which your audience will make up its mind about you, so it usually pays to start a little more slowly.

You need to 'play the odds'. Some audience members, the **graduals**, need to process information slowly, and diving in with a high impact opener and a fast pace will leave them behind, feeling overwhelmed and uncomfortable. Others, the **rapids**, process information extremely quickly. They like the high velocity, hit-and-run style opening, but they can cope with a bit of slow, as long as it doesn't go on too long and start to bore them.

Making your platform your own

At the beginning, you need to start to 'own' your platform. It is a space and you must dominate it. When you come on, put down any props you have carried in and take charge. A powerful technique to help you do this is to imagine that you and your energy occupy a bubble, like a soap bubble, which surrounds you. As you take your stage, imagine that bubble steadily growing to fill all the space on the platform. Why stop there? Let it expand further to push back and then encompass the first row of your audience, the second … all the way to the back. When you have this sense, people will read it as charisma.

Use what is often called the **lighthouse technique**, to scan across your audience, catching individuals' eyes and holding contact for two or three seconds before moving on. This gives audience members the uncanny and intimate sensation that you are talking directly to them.

Speaker's checklist: openers

Here is a list of 20 alternative ways to open your talk.

1 State something familiar – then undermine it.
2 Make a bold claim for your talk – which you *can* deliver on.
3 Assert something surprising.
4 Make a provocative remark.
5 Make a paradoxical statement.
6 Offer a prize for something.
7 Ask your audience a question.
8 Give your audience a short quiz.
9 Take a poll (show of hands) of your audience.
10 Ask for someone who fits a description – the characteristics will be relevant to your talk.
11 Tell a story – real life or allegorical.
12 Use state elicitation – get your audience into a mood or emotional state.
13 Describe a common experience that your audience will share.
14 Describe a scenario and ask a question, such as 'What would you do?'
15 Challenge your audience.
16 Recount a current or recent news story – which you will show is relevant.
17 Quote a quotation.

How to Speak so People Listen

18 Make a demonstration – call for a volunteer first to really get them on edge.

19 Draw an analogy between something familiar and your topic.

20 Make a humorous observation – but be very careful with jokes unless you are very accomplished.

Middle: impactful delivery

I am going to assume that you have designed a compelling, persuasive and powerful talk to engage and hold your audience. But how can you deliver it to maximise the impact that it has? You have five assets that can enhance (or undermine) your delivery:

1 Verbal delivery – your words.

2 Rhetorical delivery – the patterns of your speech.

3 Vocal delivery – your voice.

4 Physical delivery – your posture, gesture and expression.

5 Speakers' aids – anything you bring with you to add to you and your voice.

Verbal delivery

The words you choose are important – and we spoke a little about them earlier in this chapter, under 'style'. Choose natural, everyday language where you can, using simple words that everyone in your audience will understand straight away. Also use:

→ **Sensory language:** This is the language of seeing, hearing, touching, feeling, smelling and tasting. It makes it easy for your audience to conjure up powerful mental images and will distinguish you from the bland or confusing speakers who stick to abstract conceptual language and **management-speak**.

→ **Positive language:** Saying what you mean makes it quicker for your audience to understand you than if you tell them it's not what it isn't. And if that sounds a bit confusing … that's my point. It takes our brains just a little longer to process 'not unhealthy' than to process 'healthy'. That eats into your audience's comprehension and their eagerness to listen.

→ **Powerful language:** In Chapter 5 (page 84), we saw how some special words have great power. Add people's names to that list. When you are speaking and interacting with an audience, using audience members' names can really get people listening. Finally, some of the most powerful language of all is no words at all: silence.

Rhetorical delivery

The section on style earlier in this chapter offered you a brief introduction to the power of rhetoric to build rhythm and timing into your speech, with repetition, contrast and threes. Careful use of linking to build connections back to earlier parts of your talk also serves to underline its coherence and build a larger pattern, which audiences find appealing.

It is perhaps ironic that rhetorical questions have less rhetorical power than real questions, when you pause your delivery to ask a question of your audience, and wait for an answer. Why is this?

When you ask a question, your audience immediately processes it as a need to pay greater attention and search for an answer. Not answering it yourself – as you would with a rhetorical question – adds to the pressure on your audience to pay attention. When you invite someone else to answer, many of your audience will listen hard to compare their own answers to the ones given, heightening attention again. And when you resume speaking, the audience has had a break from your voice and listens to you with renewed alertness.

Vocal delivery

Your voice is like a musician's instrument or a carpenter's tools – it is the immediate means by which speakers do their job. Yet how many of us take the time to hone it? Professional voice coaches, whether in acting, singing or voice-over, identify many ways to vary your voice. Putting them together will make your voice a rich and powerful tool.

Speaker's checklist: voice – ten things you can vary

1 **Pace or speed:** Slow down for emphasis, speed up to convey excitement. Many of us need to slow our day-to-day pace for public speaking. Speaking too quickly will frustrate some listeners and not give you time to vary anything else.

2 **Volume or loudness:** You need to be easy to hear without booming. Lower your voice to draw your audience in and create intimacy. Practise deep breathing so it becomes a habit when you speak. More breath means more air; more air means louder volume.

3 **Pitch or tone:** The lower end of your register carries more weight, and variety keeps you interesting. Tone primarily carries emotional cues.

4 **Modulation – how pitch varies through a sentence:** Go up at the end for a question, down at the end to deliver a powerful point. Flat tone throughout is monotonous and ambiguous.

5 **Cadence or inflection – how pitch varies through a word:** Use inflection to add particular stress and interest to your speech.

6 **Stress or emphasis of a word or phrase:** Pick out the words that carry the burden of your message and emphasise these with pitch, pace and volume. Try repeating the following sentences, changing the word you emphasise each time. Each word can be emphasised to get a different meaning every time: 'I never said she stole that money'; 'I was born in London'.

7 **Rhythm – patterns of speed and emphasis:** Rhythm can make listening easy – sometimes too easy, when it becomes hypnotic. So vary it by varying pitch and pace.

8 **Timbre – the quality of your voice:** From nasal, to gravelly, to breathy, to raspy, to mellow, to clear, to crisp, to clipped – we all have a vocal quality, partly dictated by our physiology and partly by how we use it. Breathing and facial expression are the keys to getting this right. Try saying the following sentence when smiling and then when frowning: 'I had a lovely time at your party.'

▶

9 **Locus – where you project your voice to:** Some people speak loudly yet few hear – the words get trapped in their mouth. Open your lungs and your mouth and project the sound to each corner of the room.

10 **Accent and pronunciation:** These combine many of the other factors to create a distinctive regional and social voice and speech pattern.

One of the simplest ways to introduce power to your voice is to increase your use of pauses. They create tension and give your audience time to consider what you have said. They also slow you down and give the impression of a deeper tone to your voice, thus conveying greater authority. Practise mentally counting 'one, two' at the end of each sentence to get a feel for how much to allow at the end of a 'standard' sentence. Use a longer pause – or indeed a shorter one – to create a specific effect.

Developing your voice is a whole study in itself and there are many excellent books and courses that can help you. They will give you exercises to address all the ways you can develop your voice.

Physical delivery

Your body posture can be a direct give-away of your mental state. We have already considered eye-contact, and you know that smiling will not only portray warmth and confidence but also improve the quality of your voice, but how about the way you stand?

That question, by the way, implies that you are going to stand. That should be your default: it gives you more height, opens out your chest for greater breath volume and portrays confidence and respect.

The best posture is upright, with your back neither arched nor hunched. Stand facing your audience, square on to them. Keep your posture as symmetric as you can, because asymmetry is often read unconsciously as a sign of discomfort or even deception. Here are a few more things to beware of:

→ **Hand-cuffs:** Holding your hands rigidly together to still a fidget is just as distracting as fidgeting.

→ **Fig leaf:** Avoid standing with your hands together in front of your genital area.

- → **Pockets:** Hands in pockets work for some speakers, but not all. If you must do it, empty your pockets first and keep your hands still inside them.

- → **Crossed feet:** Not only does this look precarious (or that you are in a hurry to get to a bathroom); it is unstable. Women do this a lot. Feet hip-width apart is stable and looks good. If you want to come across as more dominant, go for shoulder width.

- → **Cuffs and collars:** Playing with your cuffs or your collar and tie for men, or your bracelet or necklace for women will make you look nervous.

The flip side of this is the use of deliberate gestures to convey emotion and enhance the impact of your words. If you gesture with your arms, make the movements echo your words. For example, spell out a sequence of three points on your fingers, or gesture from right to left to signify the passing of time. Think about that second one: in the West we tend to picture time as moving from left to right. When you gesture right to left, your audience sees left to right. Very few speakers do this, but when they get it right it is very powerful.

POOR SPEAKER POSTURE

Speakers' aids

This book is called *How to Speak so People Listen*, so visual aids and demonstrations are pretty much out of its scope. However, I do want to make a few points and give you a few tips.

Firstly, visual aids should be visual *aids*. Don't let them dominate, and make sure they help you. And by help you, I mean help you to communicate – use them to support your audience in hearing, understanding and remembering your message. They are not to support you in remembering your speech or the three points you wanted to make at slide six.

If you are using projected images, what I suggest is that you keep the words on your slides to an absolute minimum, and use strong and relevant images that either help understanding (such as diagrams), reinforce memory (such as powerful photographs) or simply entertain (such as cartoons). If your slide contains a lot of information, such as a graph or a long quotation, here is how I would present it:

1 Signpost what is coming up, using words only, so that your audience knows what it is going to see.

2 Put the slide up.

3 Saying nothing, turn to look at the slide. This will direct your audience's attention to it.

4 Continue looking at it for enough time for your audience to assimilate what is on the slide, still saying nothing.

5 Turn conspicuously to face your audience. This movement will draw their attention back to you. If you got your timing right, there will be no conflict for them over where to give their attention.

6 Now you have their whole attention, make your comments about the slide, offering interpretation, insight, explanation or challenge that adds to what they already learned from it.

Speaker's toolkit: designing effective visual aids

The two most used tools on the market for professional presentations are Microsoft's PowerPoint and Apple's Keynote, but do also consider various cloud-based options, such as Prezi or SlideRocket. Whichever you choose, the key is to use them well. Here are some tips:

→ Don't be cleverer than you need to be to communicate clearly. Fades, transitions and animations, for example, usually just detract from your speaking.

→ One idea per view.

→ More images; less text.

→ Space and emptiness is as powerful on a slide as silence is in speech.

→ Use one font (at most two) throughout and keep all text to a large enough size to be read easily from the back of a room (28pt or more). A quick test: stand two to four metres from your computer screen. If you can't read the text clearly, make it bigger.

→ Use contrasting colours for text and background, and keep backgrounds simple to avoid distracting attention.

→ The **rules of three** helps good design: 1. Divide the screen into a three by three grid; use the horizontal or vertical thirds to place objects pleasingly; 2. Never have more than three elements on an image; 3. Three similar objects will look better than two or four.

→ Use colour for interest and impact. Adopt a colour theme for text and graphics, using house styles rigorously where you have them. Avoid using red, orange and green to draw distinctions – an inability to distinguish these is the commonest form of colour-blindness.

→ Learn how different colours are interpreted. This is culturally determined and varies from country to country. In the UK black = authority, dark blue = trustworthy, yellow = optimism, purple = creative, red = risk and excitement. And learn what colours work well together and which ones clash. Adobe's Kuler web app (and others like it) is a great asset in creating pleasing colour combinations.

→ Simplify charts and diagrams to carry one clear message, and optimise layout, colour and labelling to make your message easy to assimilate.

→ Always proofread at least two days after you created your slides – and get someone else to do it too.

End: closing

The end of your speech, talk or presentation gives you the opportunity to achieve three things:

Pathos

Use the power of emotion to strengthen the impact of your message. Tell a brief story, conjure up some consequences of either action or inaction, or use a telling quote, for example.

Summarise

Summarise what you have said, giving the chance to use 'recency' to nail memorability one last time.

Now is the time to give a clear, easy-to-remember summary. Can you do it in three points? Can you use a rhetorical technique, like alliteration, rhyme or two things similar then one different, to make them sound good? Can you do it in under a minute? If you can do all these, your summary will stick, and your audience will be ready for your final …

Call to action

Give a short rallying call to tell your audience what they must do next; the simpler and sooner the better.

Speaker's checklist: closers

I have grouped my examples of closers under the three components mentioned above, but with some creativity, many can be adapted to other purposes.

Pathos

1 Tell a story.

2 Give a personal anecdote.

3 Use a quotation.

4 Close a loop – finish a story that you started earlier on and left unfinished. Alternatively, offer the moral of a story you told earlier.

5 Summon up an emotional state in your audience.

6 Describe what it will feel like when the audience has made the change (which you will reiterate in your call to action).

How to Speak so People Listen

7 Ask a rhetorical question, and answer it with an easy-to-remember answer.

8 Do or say something unexpected – then explain the relevance.

Summaries

9 Make three simple points.

10 List the benefits or valuable applications of what you have said.

11 Use counterpoint: this, not that.

12 Restate the problem and then your solution.

13 State how your points prove your argument.

14 Make a clear and definitive statement.

15 Link back to your opening.

16 Transform your central idea into a simple slogan.

Calls to action

17 Make a conditional close: 'If this; then that.'

18 Give instructions – in steps.

19 Lay down a challenge to your audience.

All three in one

20 Repeat a word or phrase in three consecutive sentences, for example: 'It's been a pleasure to speak to you today. It's been a pleasure to put forward some exciting ideas for you. And I'm certain it will be a pleasure to for us all to see the results next year. Thank you!'

Handling questions and challenges

So it's over: you have given your speech, made your presentation or done your talk. But oh, one moment, the audience has questions.

Handling questions

Let's start with a simple four-step approach to handling a question.

Step 1: Listen intently to the question, turning your whole body towards the questioner and approaching them if the space allows. Use good eye-contact and good listening.

Step 2: If you have not got it already, get their name, and thank them for their question.

Step 3: Repeat the question back to check your understanding; first use the same key words and phrases that they used and then restate it in your terms to confirm that you understand what they want to know or the point they have made.

Step 4: SCOPE the question: **stop**, **clarify** if you need to, think of **options** for how to respond, **proceed** and **evaluate** your response by observing reactions and asking for feedback.

Handling tough questions

If the question was in the form of a challenge or a disagreement, always start by highlighting where you agree, so narrowing down the scope of the disagreement. Then clarify whether it is the underlying facts, the method of analysis or the interpretation that you disagree on. The rest, you can bank as agreement. The more you agree on, the easier it will be to build rapport.

If you are with a colleague and you need help, flag up your need without dumping them in a hole: say something like 'Thank you for your question. In a moment I will ask my colleague for her views, but let me give you my thoughts first.' This will give your colleague a chance to think through their response.

In the absence of a colleague, you might do the same, but throw it open to the rest of the audience. This is especially helpful if you suspect the questioner is making mischief or just not getting it.

You may, by the way, recognise that they are right and you were wrong. In this case, there is only one approach: admit it, thank them and modify your position.

Handling resistance

Sometimes, however, you will be right, and yet an audience member will resist your answer. If this happens, stay calm and listen carefully to what they say. Use this to diagnose the nature of their resistance, and respond appropriately. You will find an analysis of the six principal types of resistance, and how to deal with each one, in my short book *The Handling Resistance Pocketbook*.

The YES/NO of public speaking

YES

→ Give your presentation PEP: passion, energy and poise.

→ Prepare mentally and physically, and rehearse often.

→ Accept nerves as meaning you are properly excited.

→ Make use of pauses and silence.

→ Start slowly.

→ Vary the pitch, pace and loudness of your voice.

→ Close with pathos, summary and a call to action.

NO

→ Avoid reading anything, except direct quotations.

→ Don't let your visual aids dominate – they should be an aid to your audience in enjoying, understanding or remembering what you say.

→ The same goes for your clothes and accessories – don't let them be more interesting than your presentation or speech.

→ Don't get fazed by difficult questions. Stay calm and respectful, and SCOPE the question.

Final insights

Part Four

The 25 core concepts of How to Speak so People Listen

Chapter Eleven

How to Speak so People Listen is written around 25 core concepts that I have developed over the last few years. Well, to be honest, I didn't develop all of them: some of them I inherited from other, greater, thinkers than myself, and some I synthesised from lots of ideas.

All these ideas are interconnected, so there is no single route through them all. Writing any book – even a non-fiction business-oriented book like this one – is a task in creating a linear narrative through many complex and interdependent ideas. If I have created a compelling structure that has made sense to you, then I have, in that small part at least, succeeded.

The figure on the opposite page shows how these 25 core concepts connect to each other, and the numbering sets out the route I will take in summarising this whole book in 25 short paragraphs.

To make complete sense of this, you will, of course, need to refer to the figures in the book and read the relevant sections. But do not for one minute think that the spaces between these core concepts in this 50,000-word book are mere filler. I have worked hard to make every single word of this book count. There are many, many gems of tips and advice for you. These are just my personal top 25 ideas.

So, on with the task my editor set me: to write a short summary of a long book …

1 Communication and response

When we formulate and communicate an idea, what matters most is the response we get. We need to notice that response and adjust our approach accordingly if it is not what we expected or wanted (see the figure on page 8).

Speaker's insight: Great speakers take responsibility for the way their audiences respond to them. Response and responsibility come from the same root.

2 The six levels of speaking

Speaking so that people listen is only the first of six levels of speaking that this book addresses. The book is far more ambitious than that, and ranges up to level six (see the figure on page 12):

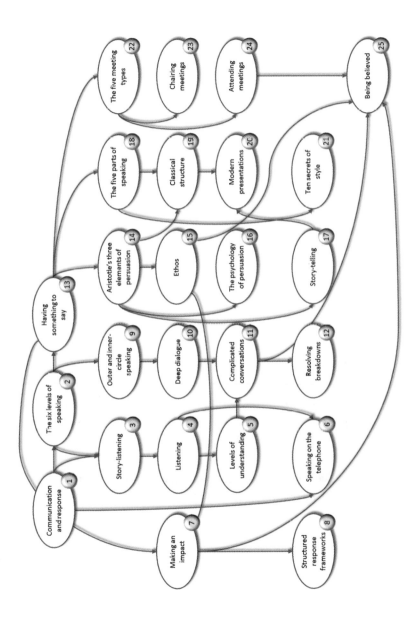

Level 1: How to speak so people listen.

Level 2: How to speak so people understand.

Level 3: How to speak so people understand, as you intend them to.

Level 4: How to speak so people agree with you.

Level 5: How to speak so people remember what you want them to.

Level 6: How to speak so people think or do what want them to.

Speaker's insight: Make your speaking compelling, to address levels 1 and 2; make it persuasive, to address levels 3 and 4; and make it powerful, if you want to address levels 5 and 6 and create real change.

3 Story-listening

When you listen to someone speak, your brain filters what you hear and turns it into a story, which is just your representation of what the speaker intends. The closer your story is to matching the speaker's, the more effective the communication process (see the figure on page 15).

Speaker's insight: We don't act on what other people say, but on how we feel about what we think they said. This separation is the big challenge that speakers really face.

4 Listening

We naturally listen at four different levels: from the most superficial, pretending, through selecting, to attending to the deepest level, empathising. To get the best from people, follow the ten-step process for deep, attentive listening (see page 120).

Speaker's insight: The main reason why most people do not listen well is simple: if you want to listen well, you must care – you must want to hear what they have to say.

5 Levels of understanding

When we listen, we understand what we hear at different levels. Your speaking power arises from how you affect others' understanding at all the levels; not just the most superficial surface level, but all the way down to the depths of my needs, feelings and who I think I am (see the figure on page 91).

Speaker's insight: Most of our understanding is at a superficial level, based on the words we hear. True speaking power extends well beyond just sparking people's interest: speaking power = interest + insight + influence + impact + impulsion + inspiration.

6 Speaking on the telephone

Good practice in speaking on the phone follows the same rules as a face-to-face conversation. There are, however a number of powerful tips for planning your calls, picking up a call, during the call, ending a call and your follow-up, after the call. Find out more in the checklist on page 123.

Speaker's insight: It is so easy to do something else while you are on the phone – and so tempting, with all the pressures on your time. If the call matters – don't. Focus on one thing only: your conversation. If the call doesn't matter, politely excuse yourself and get on with that other thing, giving that all your attention instead.

7 Making an impact

People will only listen to you if you can get their attention and hold it. This means making a positive impact: a combination of posture, positioning, presence and making a clear proposition in your opening words. This is the subject of Chapter 4.

Speaker's insight: The work of Amy Cuddy and her colleagues underscores how important your mental and emotional state is, and how profoundly it is linked to your physicality. Upright, assertive and even dominant postures do help you to make an impact.

8 Structured response frameworks

When you are called upon to say something of value with little preparation – most often in response to something that has just happened or just been said – putting your thoughts into a logical and clear structure will mightily increase your impact. The 'Speaker's toolkit' on page 65 contains eight simple frameworks for structured responses that should cover pretty much every eventuality.

Speaker's insight: Less is more. When you want people to hang on your every word, give your words rarity value. Speak only when you are asked or have something insightful to say, and put it into a few short, clear sentences that build logically on one another. Then stop and shut up, displaying confidence that there is nothing more you need to say.

9 Outer and inner-circle speaking

We can speak in superficial terms using clichés and euphemisms that hide what we really think and feel, or we can reveal our true thoughts and feelings. These are outer and inner-circle speaking, respectively (see the figure on page 129).

Speaker's insight: Say what you mean and mean what you say. If you say less, then make sure it comes directly from the core of your thinking, so you can communicate things that really matter.

10 Deep dialogue

When two people speak to one another from their inner circles and each listens with intense attention, this creates a deep dialogue that can have tremendous power to influence and change us (see the figure on page 140).

Speaker's insight: A free flow of information is essential for good decision making – and when you speak, you want to influence my decisions. Invite people into a deep dialogue to build conversations that create change.

11 Complicated conversations

Complicated conversations are characterised by important consequences, complexity, emotional baggage and a host of other features.
You know them when you get into one. Chapter 8 focuses on these
uncomfortable features of our lives and includes a seven-step process
for facilitating them (see page 142).

Speaker's insight: When we focus on the past we find reasons to blame, and when
we focus on the present we see only the motives and values of the people around
us. It is when we focus on the future that we start to attend to the options and
choices from which changes can arise.

12 Resolving breakdowns

Sometimes relationships break down. If you choose to try to fix
one, there is a process that will give you structure and improve your
chances of success (see the figure on page 151).

Speaker's insight: When an important relationship has broken down, both
parties know it but are often afraid to say so out loud. Resolution can only start
when one of you has the courage to say 'Something has gone wrong, and I truly
want to fix it'.

13 Having something to say

Who would want to listen to you speaking if you did not have something worthwhile to say? Nobody. You need find a reason to speak
and something interesting to say. So Chapter 3 focuses on how to get
something to say.

Speaker's insight: Often the most interesting things are new perspectives on
something familiar. Consider the subject you want to talk about, and synthesise
different ideas you encounter with each other and with your own ideas, to find a new
way of speaking about a familiar topic.

14 Aristotle's three elements of persuasion

As often happens, the ancient Greeks got there first – in this case with how to make a persuasive case. Aristotle told us it needs to demonstrate three things: the depth of your character – why I should listen to *you*, the logic of your case – why I should *agree* with you, and the power of your arguments to move me *emotionally*. As you'd expect, these have Greek names too: **ethos**, **logos** and **pathos** – see page 75 to find out more.

Speaker's insight: Have you ever made a point and known you were right, yet found that people didn't agree with you? We often do. This is the weakness of logos when it is alone. It is ethos and pathos that make a strong argument compelling and persuasive.

15 Ethos

Ethos is the proper Greek word for the first of Aristotle's three elements: character. Demonstrating ethos is showing why I should believe *you* – *your* credibility. There are seven ways to build this credibility – and they all start with the letter C, as you'll learn in the 'Speaker's checklist' on page 76.

Speaker's insight: One of the strongest reasons that I should find you credible is if I believe you are like me and share my concerns, my values and my opinions. This is why politicians spend so much time trying to demonstrate how much they are like their target voter.

16 The psychology of persuasion

Modern psychologists have been formalising and testing the methods people have used to influence and persuade for centuries. There are lots of techniques, all of which create ethos and pathos. I have summarised six of the most valuable to speakers on page 100.

Speaker's insight: One simple piece of psychology trumps all others: self-interest. You can make your persuasion task a whole lot easier if you can answer that simple question that is going through my mind: 'What's in it for me?'

17 Story-telling

Nothing is as good at pulling our emotional strings as a good story, so your ability to create and tell one well will give you a real boost as a speaker to whom people want to listen. Stories fill every culture, but many follow one of a relatively small number of plots. There is a list of some common ones in the 'Speaker's checklist' of 14 basic plots on page 73.

Speaker's insight: The best speakers are 'story magpies' – always on the alert for a good story that they can adapt for their own use, and changing characters and details not just to avoid copying the original but to make it more resonant to their audience. Many of the examples in this book started as stories I heard while consulting with clients or speaking with colleagues.

18 The five parts of speaking

The ancient Roman orators divided the art of public speaking, rhetoric, into five parts. Who am I to do differently? So, having focused on **invention** and **arrangement** in Chapters 3 and 5 respectively, Chapter 10 contains sections on **style**, **memory** and **delivery**.

Speaker's insight: Classical and medieval students, merchants, lawyers and politicians spent many years studying how to speak effectively: how much time have you spent? If you have spent years learning your professional or business skills, ask yourself how important being heard and being able to influence are to your future success. Have you given the craft of speaking enough attention? I doubt it.

19 Classical structure

Classical education taught a structure for the arrangement of your speech that was favoured by the great Roman lawyer and orator Cicero. This classical six-part structure – of introduction, narration, division, proof, refutation and conclusion – is described in Chapter 5, on page 61.

Speaker's insight: Good structures work because they address all the needs of a speaker who wants people to listen: they start by establishing ethos, create a compelling sequence, provide for persuasive logical arguments, and build in a powerful ending that harnesses our emotional responses.

20 Modern presentations

For modern business audiences, you are far more likely to be making a presentation than a speech. So Chapter 5 also contains a structure for these and describes how the best way to create your presentation follows a different sequence, starting with the most important parts (see the figure on page 68).

Speaker's insight: Most people start preparing their presentations by drawing the title slide of the PowerPoint or Keynote deck. Then they work through, logically, from slide two, to three, to … Don't do this. Start by writing down your central idea: the one message you want your audience to hear, understand, remember and even act on. Build your presentation around that.

21 Ten secrets of style

One of the five parts of speaking is style, and there are ten secrets, which together contribute to your compelling, persuasive and powerful speech, presentation or comments. See what they are on page 179.

Speaker's insight: If I were to choose one of the ten secrets of style to emphasise, it would be stories. Tell a story and make it personal to your audience. Create characters and situations that reflect their own lives, fears or aspirations. Stories just work – because humans are story-telling creatures.

22 The five meeting types

Meetings are nothing more than a series of conversations, and there are five types of conversation. In fact there are many different types of meeting, as you can combine these five conversation types into a sequence, and because few meetings have just one purpose. But hey – this is just a heading. The five are conversations for possibility, opportunity, action, relationships and ritual, and you can find out more about them on page 160 of Chapter 9.

Speaker's insight: Conversations for ritual happen because they seem to have always happened – often for longer than anyone can remember. Nobody enjoys them, few people get anything out of them at all, yet nobody has the courage to say 'This emperor has no clothes'. Drop them, avoid them, or, better yet, still turn up and then declare them a waste of time.

23 Chairing meetings

The quality of a meeting and how much of value it can achieve are often down to how well it is chaired. You will need to think about preparing, conducting and following up the meeting, and I have given you plenty of valuable checklists and toolkits to help you in Chapter 9.

Speaker's insight: If you are in the chair, you control not just what the meeting talks about, but also the moods of the participants. People will look to you to take their lead, so choose your mental state with care. As you go through the door, put your anger, frustration, disappointment or any other negative emotion to one side, and adopt the emotions that will get the best from your meeting. These emotions could be curiosity, enchantment, pleasure, enthusiasm, hope or determination.

24 Attending meetings

As a speaker who attends meetings, you will want people to listen to your contributions. You will find advice on how to make your contributions count, starting on page 167 of Chapter 9.

Speaker's insight: Treat a meeting like a good magazine: everything can interest you, but listen for the one or two nuggets that can change the way you think, can prompt a change of direction or can help you solve the problem you have.

25 Being believed

Do you ever need people to believe you? I hope it is only when you are telling the truth, but whether it is in a conversation, a meeting or in a court of law, there are steps you can take, attitudes you can choose and body language you can adopt that will make you more believable. And yes, these are things that lawyers tell vital witnesses to learn. Get them here, on page 171.

Speaker's insight: As is often the case, this ultimate test of ethos is less about what you say and more about how you say it. Slow down, answer the question you are asked and not what you think you should have been asked, give no more than you are asked and avoid speculating. When you have answered the question, stop – don't let the silence tempt you to add to your answer: this is what tends to undermine your credibility.

Closing words

If you have a voice, you have a right to speak. But this does not mean that people have an obligation to listen to you.

If you want people to listen, if you want to be heard – that is a privilege that you have to earn. Everyone can earn that privilege if they put in the work. To earn it, you must:

→ Do the work it takes to create something of value to say.

→ Find a way to say it in an engaging way.

→ Give your audience the respect they deserve.

→ Make the effort to speak clearly and compellingly.

If you have something to say, silence will not be an option for you. That would be cowardice. Yet some conversations, we know, are complicated, difficult and uncomfortable. They take courage. Prepare well and summon that courage because, for a person of integrity, they are an obligation.

There will always be risk when you express yourself. No amount of preparation can determine what a listener will hear when you speak. But prepare well, treat people with respect and speak from your inner circle. If you do that, you will speak with integrity.

However people choose to react to that, they will listen.

Speak well, and be heard.

Who else needs to speak so people listen?

We all know people who would want to be more effective speakers. Who do you know, who could benefit from *How to Speak so People Listen*?

Will you recommend it?

Will you buy them their own copy?

Will you lend them yours?

… or will you give yours away?

Mike can speak so your audience listens

 Mike is a conference speaker and business consultant. He speaks at conferences, team events, workshops and seminars for companies, associations, public authorities and not-for-profit organisations. Mike also offers one-to-one and small group coaching for people who want to speak so people listen.

Mike's topics include management and leadership, project management and the management of change, wisdom, and personal effectiveness. You can book Mike to talk about *How to Speak so People Listen* or another topic at **www.mikeclayton.co.uk** or **www.speaksopeoplelisten.co.uk**

Also by Mike Clayton

Mike Clayton is author of nine other books to date:

The Yes/No Book: How to Do Less ... and Achieve More,
Pearson, 2012

Smart to Wise: The Seven Pillars for True Success, Marshall
Cavendish, 2012

*Brilliant Project Leader: What the Best Project Leaders Know,
Do and Say to Get Results, Every Time*, Pearson, 2012

*Brilliant Stress Management: How to Manage Stress in Any
Situation*, Pearson, 2011

*Risk Happens! Managing Risk and Avoiding Failure in Business
Projects*, Marshall Cavendish, 2011

*Brilliant Time Management: What the Most Productive People
Know, Do and Say*, Pearson, 2011

*Brilliant Influence: What the Most Influential People Know, Do and
Say*, Pearson, 2010

The Handling Resistance Pocketbook, Management Pocketbooks,
2010

The Management Models Pocketbook, Management Pocketbooks,
2009

Learn more

Some books you might enjoy, and that will extend your understanding of some of the topics in *How to Speak so People Listen*:

Appreciative Inquiry for Change Management: Using AI to Facilitate Organizational Development by Sarah Lewis, Jonathan Passmore, and Stefan Cantore, Kogan Page, 2011

The Book of Tells by Peter Collett, Bantam, 2004

Brilliant Influence: What the Most Influential People Know, Do and Say by Mike Clayton, Pearson, 2010

The Five Paths to Persuasion: The Art of Selling Your Message by Robert B Miller, Gary A Williams and Alden M Hayashi, Kogan Page, 2007

The Handling Resistance Pocketbook by Mike Clayton, Management Pocketbooks, 2010

How to Talk to Anyone: 92 Little Tricks For Big Success in Relationships by Leil Lowndes, Thorsons, 2008

Lend Me Your Ears: All You Need to Know About Making Speeches and Presentations by Max Atkinson, Vermillion, 2004

The Mind Map Book: Unlock Your Creativity, Boost Your Memory, Change Your Life by Tony Buzan, BBC Active, 2009

The Presentation Secrets of Steve Jobs: How to Be Insanely Great in Front of Any Audience by Carmine Gallo, McGraw-Hill Professional, 2009

What Every Body Is Saying: An Ex-FBI Agent's Guide to Speed-Reading People by Joe Navarro, HarperCollins, 2008

Your Voice and How to Use It by Cicely Berry, Virgin Books, 2000

Index